Physical Characteristics of the Shetland Sheepdog
(from the American Kennel Club breed standard)

Body: Back should be level and strongly muscled. Chest should be deep, the brisket reaching to point of elbow. The ribs should be well sprung, but flattened at their lower half to allow free play of the foreleg and shoulder. Abdomen moderately tucked up.

Tail: Sufficiently long so that when it is laid along the back edge of the hind legs the last vertebra will reach the hock joint. Carriage of tail at rest is straight down or in a slight upward curve.

Hindquarters: The thigh should be broad and muscular. The overall length of the stifle should at least equal the length of the thighbone, and preferably should slightly exceed it. The hock should be short and straight viewed from all angles.

Size: Between 13 and 16 inches at the shoulder.

Coat: Double, the outer coat consisting of long, straight, harsh hair; the undercoat short, furry, and so dense as to give the entire coat its "standoff" quality.

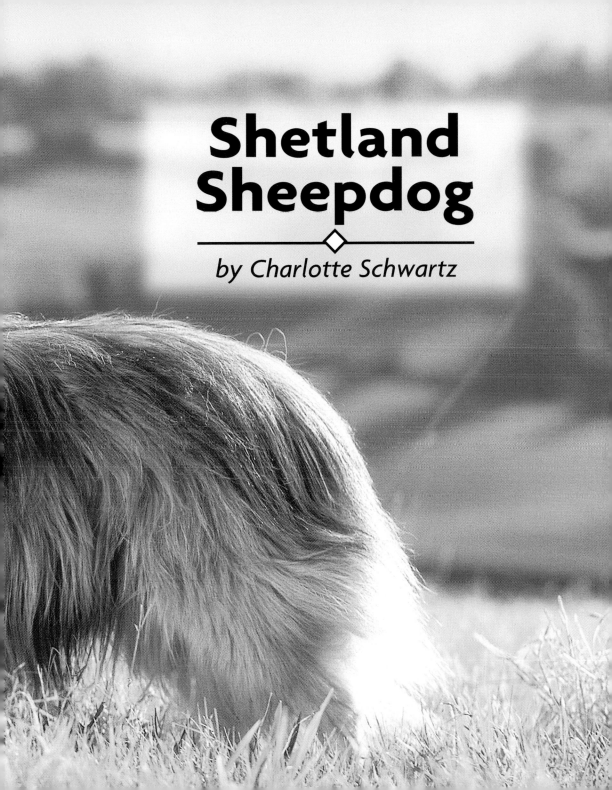

Shetland
Sheepdog

◇

by Charlotte Schwartz

9
History of the Shetland Sheepdog

Trace the beginnings of the Shetland Sheepdog as a skilled sheep-herder in the rugged Scottish mountain country and follow its spread in popularity around the world as a companion dog, show dog, competition dog and ambassador of canine good will.

20
Characteristics of the Shetland Sheepdog

Friendly, outgoing and intelligent, the Shetland Sheepdog is both a hard worker and a wonderful choice for a companion dog. Find out about the personality and physical characteristics of the Sheltie, as well as breed-specific health concerns.

27
Breed Standard for the Shetland Sheepdog

Learn the requirements of a well-bred Shetland Sheepdog by studying the description of the breed as set forth in the American Kennel Club's breed standard. Both show dogs and pets must possess key characteristics as outlined in the breed standard.

34
Your Puppy Shetland Sheepdog

Be advised about choosing a reputable breeder and selecting a healthy, typical puppy. Understand the responsibilities of ownership, including home preparation, acclimatization, the vet and prevention of common puppy problems.

63
Everyday Care of Your Shetland Sheepdog

Enter into a sensible discussion of dietary and feeding considerations, exercise, grooming, traveling and identification of your dog. This chapter discusses Shetland Sheepdog care for all stages of development.

80
Training Your Shetland Sheepdog

Be informed about the importance of training your Shetland Sheepdog from the basics of housebreaking and understanding the development of a young dog to executing obedience commands (sit, stay, down, etc.).

Contents

KENNEL CLUB BOOKS: **SHETLAND SHEEPDOG**
ISBN 13: 978-1-59378-232-0

Copyright © 2000, **2009** • Kennel Club Books® • A Division of BowTie, Inc.
40 Broad Street, Freehold, NJ 07728 USA
Cover Design Patented: US 6,435,559 B2 • Printed in South Korea

Photos by Carol Ann Johnson, with additional photos by:
Norvia Behling, Carolina Biological Supply, Doskocil,
Isabelle Français, James Hayden-Yoav, James R. Hayden, RBP, Joan Jenks,
Bill Jonas, Dwight R. Kuhn, Dr. Dennis Kunkel, Mikki Pet Products,
Phototake, Jean Claude Revy, Charlotte Schwartz,
Dr. Andrew Spielman, Karen Taylor, and C. James Webb.
Illustrations by Patricia Peters.

Special thanks to Sandrine Altier, Agnès Falleri, John J. Gorman, Muriel Jochem,
Emeric L'Esterazur du Lac, Laura Parker, Nancy Runyon, Cecile Sibilia, Charlette Thebault,
Mrs. Tinker, Shirley Vicchitto, Kathy D. Ziegel and all owners of dogs featured in this book.

HISTORY OF THE

SHETLAND SHEEPDOG

Stand atop a hillside overlooking an emerald valley. Feel the soft summer breeze rising up from the land below to bring you the scent of green grass and lush vegetation. Scan the valley that runs for several miles beneath you. Notice the beige cloud that slowly undulates across the valley, then look again.

It's not a cloud. It's a flock of hundreds of sheep moving as one across the field. Wonder now at what keeps them together and forces them to move in such beautiful symmetry. Focus on the sheep cloud as your eyes adjust to the scene. Only then will you notice two small dark creatures around the outside of the flock.

Those dark specks are Shetland Sheepdogs, developed for use in the Shetland Islands off the northern coast of Scotland. The dogs are doing what they've been doing for hundreds of years: keeping the flock together and guiding the path of its travel. They are herding sheep.

They take directions from a distant herdsman who whistles his orders to them. The sound of his whistling starts and stops the

dogs, turns them backwards and forwards, right and left. He often directs them to go fetch a stray ewe as she wanders away from the flock.

As you watch the dogs work, marvel at the wonder of these small creatures handling hundreds of sheep, each of which weighs many times more than a Shetland Sheepdog.

Now wonder no more: Here within these pages is the story of how and why these little dogs manage such great feats. Their story truly is remarkable, considering that they are descended from the great strong collies of ancient Scotland.

This whole Shetland thing began thousands of years ago in the rugged mountain country of Scotland known as the Highlands. It is the dogs' skill and intelligence at handling animals such as sheep, cattle and reindeer that fostered their development and has sustained them as unsurpassed herders, even into the 21st century.

Lacking authentic historical records regarding the origin of Shetland Sheepdogs, we are left

Opposite page: Aside from being a magnificent, beautiful representative of the dog world, the Shetland Sheepdog is a warm, loving pet for millions of homes around the world.

The Shetland
Sheepdog,
though originally
bred for herding
sheep, has also
shown great
skills and
aptitude in
herding cattle.

to take bits and pieces of information—stories, occasional written references, paintings, old
tales passed from one generation
to the next—to recreate a most
probable scenario for the breed's
beginning. Thus goes the story.

As far back as Neolithic
times, 3500 to 2000 BC, there
were collie-type northern sheepdogs that were finding their way
south into the Mediterranean
countries. From there, they eventually traveled with merchant
traders to the British Isles.

Going back even further, we
find that these collie-type dogs
descended from northern Euro-
pean and Asian wolves, thus
making the dogs genetically
predisposed to herding and

manipulating large flocks of
animals. Wolves obtain food by
using this method of rounding
up their prey in order to pick out
a candidate for the kill. The
collie-type dogs of today therefore still carry within their genes
the traits for herding.

In addition, modern collie-
type dogs rely on a master, a
human, to oversee their work.
This trait comes from the original wolves that needed an alpha
wolf to guide them in the
roundup and the hunt. Absent a
leader, neither the wolves of
ancient times nor the dogs of
today would survive and pros-
per. Both are social animals.

About the time that the
collie-type dogs were settling in

England and Scotland, the farmers of the Shetland Islands, known as crofters, were using dogs to herd their flocks of sheep. They paid little attention to the size and uniformity of the dogs—they were concerned only with the dogs' ability to work.

However, when they visited the mountainous Highlands of Scotland, they became fascinated with the large collies of the mainland. The intelligence and dedication of those big dogs were qualities much desired in working dogs, and the Shetland Islanders began using them to improve and refine their own "toonies" or local "township" dogs.

Scottish, Dutch and Scandinavian fishermen also stopped at the Shetland Islands with some frequency. Occasionally they brought with them dogs they kept on board their vessels. On one occasion, as an old yarn tells us, a yacht touched the island and on board was a black-and-tan King Charles Spaniel. This dog eventually bred with some of the island dogs, thus launching the true beginning of the Shetland Sheepdogs.

Their size was the only problem. Shetland sheep are about one-half the size of the black-faced sheep of Scotland. The Islanders realized from the beginning that they needed smaller collie-type dogs than those found

The black-and-tan King Charles Spaniel has been associated in folk legend with having been introduced into the bloodlines to create the Shetland Sheepdog.

in the Highlands. Thus they chose the smallest Scottish dogs to breed to their own toonies. Eventually, they produced very small collie-type dogs that they named Shetland Sheepdogs.

The end result produced a dog of distinction. The Sheltie, as it became known, closely resembled a large collie in appearance, with the happy disposition and friendly characteristics of the spaniel, and the heart, stamina and dedication to master of the English Collie.

THE ISLANDS OF "TINIES"
The Shetland Islands are not just known for miniature collies. They are also known for other diminutive animals such as cattle, sheep and ponies.

Even later dogs were cross-bred with native dogs of Greenland known as Yaks. Traces of these crosses are seen today in the large erect ears and heavy coat of the Sheltie. It seems safe to say that today's Sheltie is a combination of old native island dogs, large northern Collies, spaniels and Yaks from the frigid climate of Greenland.

The earliest record of the true Shetland Sheepdog dates back to 1840 in the form of an engraving of the town of Lerwick, capital of the Shetland Islands. It shows a Shetland pony in the background and a small collie-type dog in the foreground.

Then, in 1944, a traveler to the Shetland Islands wrote an article about the local sheepdogs that herded the flocks by day, then played and slept in the house of the herdsman by night.

As time passed, the crofters began managing larger flocks that in turn required larger collie-type dogs. Collies from the mainland were again introduced to increase the size of the Shetland dogs, and it was at this time that Shetland farmers recognized the need to stabilize the size and appearance of the dogs, thus safeguarding the breeding of the Shetland Sheepdog for all time.

The dogs possessed great intelligence and stamina with fine muscular development and thick coats due to the harshness of their island environment. These traits were carefully retained while size was added to bring the dogs to the size of 15 inches or 16 inches at the shoulder.

As the breed became stable and people could accurately predict the appearance and size of the Sheltie puppies, they

Even though small in size, when compared to a Collie or another larger herding breed, the Shetland Sheepdog still can handle very large animals in its herding mode.

The Rough Collie is recognized in three colors, including sable, black and blue merle, shown here. The close relationship between Collies and Shelties is evident from the sharing of these three color varieties.

began to be exhibited at local shows in and around Lerwick. In 1906, the breed was shown for the first time at Crufts Dog Show in London, where the dog-show community enthusiastically received them. Then, in 1908, the Shetland Collie Club was founded. It wasn't until 1910 that Crufts offered a separate classification for the breed for the first time. Both Scottish and English exhibitors provided a large entry that the public immediately embraced. Shortly after that, the Ladies Kennel Association established classes for the

dogs and their popularity exploded, with entries equal to that of the regular Collies.

THE SHETLAND ISLANDS

In 1472, the Shetland Islands became officially annexed to the Scottish Crown, giving the islanders a solid connection with the mainland. Following annexation, the islanders increased their travel between their island and Scotland to a point where they began comparing farming techniques and dog-raising with their own methods.

The Shetland Sheepdog in the UK is a smaller dog with less coat and a different head piece than its American counterpart.

THE SHETLAND SURVIVES

World War I was almost the downfall of the Shetland Sheepdog. Breeding was almost completely halted and size and type were nearly lost. One breeder, however, introduced a collie crossbred into a limited breeding program, thereby preserving the uniform type of well-boned sturdiness and size into his line. This act set the uniformity for future generations despite four years of war.

In 1911, the breed crossed the Atlantic and appeared at American shows with equal enthusiasm. However, the matter of size and type still plagued the breed in America.

In 1914, the English Sheepdog Club was formed and urged the adoption of a standard for the breed that included the specification of "the general appearance of the Shetland Collie as approximately that of a show Collie in miniature, ideal height at the shoulder, 12 inches."

Later that same year, The Kennel Club joined the Scottish and English Shetland Clubs to grant the breed individual classification. Now the Shetland Sheepdog was recognized as a breed on its own, not just as a miniature Collie.

Though controversy over size continued for several decades, the matter was finally put to rest in 1929 in America. At the famous Westminster Kennel Club Dog Show, the American Shetland Sheepdog Association united with the English and Scottish clubs to describe the breed as "resembling a Collie (Rough) in miniature" with size being designated as 12 to 15 inches at the shoulder, the ideal being 13.5 inches. Eventually, the American Shetland Sheepdog Association changed their standard to read "between 13 and 16 inches" with disqualification of any height above or below that range.

The difference of an inch or two in the size of the Shetland Sheepdog is certainly secondary to its fundamental character. Molded by the rugged land from which it came, the dog is a hard worker despite the rigors of the island's climate. His traits of intelligence, agility, soundness and dedication come from his relative, the large Collie. His love of master and family, his instinct

Erect ears that tip forward are a hallmark that is shared between the Shetland Sheepdog and the Collie. In general appearance and color as well as expression, the two breeds are remarkably similar.

to guard and protect and his sweetness of disposition, together with his fondness of the outdoors, come from his spaniel and herding progenitors. These traits remain true and obvious even today and are what make the Sheltie a dog of distinction.

Proof of the continuity of these traits lies in the fact that

THE FIRST MILLION

"Lord Scott" was the first Sheltie registered with the American Kennel Club in 1911. "Sheltieland Alice Grey Gown" was the one-millionth Sheltie registered in 1935.

The Smooth Collie is one of the Shetland Sheepdog's close relatives. Of the two Collies, the Smooth is much less popular than the Rough. Shelties cannot be smooth-coated.

the Sheltie is still used today for herding and droving in the British Isles, the Shetland Islands and America. Sheep-growers in the western United States—Montana, Utah, Colorado and Idaho, for example—employ Shelties because they cover ground so well and experience little difficulty in working in snow country. Their light weight prevents them from sinking deep into the snow as they drive the flocks. In addition, Shelties are found to be more gentle with ewes at lambing time than some of the larger herding dogs.

Though the Shetland Sheep-dog is an ancient breed, as evidenced by literature and art, the breed has managed to keep up with its master's changing lifestyles. A perfect example of this modern Sheltie phenomenon is a lovely little bitch named Tassie. Her story exemplifies the intelligence and versatility of Shelties and epitomizes the dogs' dedication to their masters.

Today Tassie lives in the tropical state of Florida with her owner, Bert Jenks. Until she retired, Tassie's life was anything but casual or leisurely. Jenks and his wife, Joan, lived on a 36,000-acre ranch in the rolling hills of central Colorado at the foot of the Rocky Mountains in the western US. Rolling High Jenks Ranch was a 52-square-mile cattle ranch. The mountain peaks that surround the ranch reach heights of 14,000 feet.

Tassie was purchased by the

Tassie, working a herd of yearling cattle on a ranch in Colorado. Tassie is owned by Bert Jenks.

Tassie, besides being a successful herder, is also a very beautiful dog. She resides happily with Bert and Joan Jenks in their retirement home in Florida.

Jenks in Florida, where they spend the winter months on the small island called Sanibel in the Gulf of Mexico, off Florida's western coast. When spring arrived and Tassie was a mere six months old, the Jenks packed up and returned to their cattle farm. At the time, the Jenks' house was not surrounded by a protective fence, so all manner of wildlife made a habit of foraging on the flowers in Joan's beds. Squirrels, rabbits, antelope and deer were regular unwelcome visitors.

Every day, Bert would take Tassie with him to work the cattle and whenever he was home, he and Tassie would chase off the wildlife in the garden. Out on the range, Tassie worked with a part-dingo dog named Buddy. Lessons from Buddy plus her natural instincts for herding taught Tassie how to move the cattle at the direction of the cowboys. Because of her small size, Tassie was usually assigned to work the yearling cattle, both heifers and steers. Though these animals weigh an average of 600 pounds each, Tassie quickly learned to stay out of their way while at the same time remaining close enough to move them according to the voice and hand signals of the herdsmen.

Tassie's life took on a regular rhythm of working cattle in Colorado and wintering in Florida with her owners. While in Florida, Tassie's life was not without purpose, however. She and Jenks enrolled in an obedience class and Tassie's formal education became a reality.

Following basic obedience training, Bert and Tassie moved

Shelties are easily trained for agility exercises such as the tire jump. Shelties make excellent candidates for agility and obedience trials.

up the ranks of various levels of difficulty until they reached the level known as "Skills." In the Skills class, Tassie developed distance control, hand signals, retrieving, jumping and scent discrimination, including narcotics detection. In other words, Tassie had reached the peak of canine performance and had done it with ease.

All the while Tassie was perfecting her training in winter, she continued herding cattle and chasing off wildlife around her home in summer. At night, regardless of where she was, she would sleep beside Bert's bed and keep watch over the house.

At age eight years, Tassie, along with her family, left the ranch they loved and retired to Florida. She still works out each week with her Skills class and has joined a dog-owner dance team.

Tassie proves an interesting theory: A dog with strong genetic factors for certain behaviors can be transported to an artificial environment and still exhibit those traits. Tassie, through hundreds of years of genetic breeding for herding, retains the herding instinct while at the same time adapts to a completely different lifestyle and excels at both. Further proof of the power of genetics and controlled breeding seems unnecessary.

Whether Shetland Sheepdogs are bred for showing, herding or pet life, their natural instincts remain intact.

CHARACTERISTICS OF THE
SHETLAND SHEEPDOG

The Shetland Sheepdog's unique heritage has given the breed certain qualities that endear it to modern owners around the world. As we've seen, genetics is what it's all about and the particular behavioral traits bred into the Sheltie so many years ago have given it the ability to adapt so successfully to modern-day living.

For example, their intelligence and natural tendency to obey with a minimum amount of training give them a decided advantage in today's busy lifestyle, and in various dog activities such as obedience and agility

TENDING THE FLOCK

Shelties love children and will spend their waking hours trying to gather their "flock" together in one room rather than being scattered throughout the house. Since the children of the family are the Sheltie's chosen flock, the Sheltie feels a great responsibility for their safety and keeping them close together.

competition. Their grace, speed and nimbleness carry over from their lives on the range to today's farm work and recreational activities such as agility trials, jumping and other sports. They are, in fact, one of the most popular breeds used in obedience trials.

Their watchdog instinct make them great alarm dogs around home and property, just as it did in guarding flocks against poachers and predators. Their docile nature, coupled with a keen awareness of their environment, makes them perfect family companions. Their devotion to family makes them a pleasure to live with and a joy to train.

Because of this devotion factor, Shelties are best obtained as puppies rather than as mature

Intelligence, friendly temperament, working ability and beauty— the Shetland Sheepdog is a breed that has it all.

adults since, as adults, they have most likely bonded strongly with their first owners. The transition to another owner later in life can prove extremely stressful. Sheltie owners have often told how their dogs sulk or yearn for them when they go away.

Shelties make ideal family pets and are very tolerant of all

COAT CARE
Due to the heavy coat of the Sheltie, he can withstand cold climates very easily. However, that same coat requires daily brushing and owners must expect heavy shedding at least once a year. If you don't like brushing a dog—or are allergic to dog hair— seek a different breed.

Shelties make
wonderful pets,
especially when
brought home as
a puppy and
allowed to bond
with all family
members.

Shelties make wonderful pets, especially when brought home as a puppy and allowed to bond with all family members.

calls for attention. This vocalization is best limited by teaching the dog not to bark excessively at an early age. Allow the dog to warn you of visitors to your home, but discourage unnecessary barking, for example, when he's excited about something or in anticipation of dinnertime or friends' coming by for a visit.

Shelties are busy dogs. They do not enjoy being left around the house with nothing to do or forced to be inactive for too long. In these instances, they can become distressed and neurotic. They need daily exercise and regular physical activities that get them outdoors and doing things such as hiking, walking in the park, jogging with owners, etc. Remember, this is a dog bred to run for miles each day without tiring; a two-mile run will hardly be considered a challenge!

children. Actually, they love little children and usually watch over them as would a nanny. Owners must be mindful, however, of infants and toddlers who may wobble and fall on the dog, causing injury to the dog.

Owners will often observe their Sheltie trying to round up the children as if they were his own little flock of sheep! The Sheltie likes to see his human family members clustered together rather than separated and apart from one another.

Shelties can also be very vocal. With a high-pitched bark they express frustrations, concern, excitement and even

A HERD OF BIRDS?

In many countries, young Shelties are first trained to herd on ducks. Since the ducks easily cluster together and can be moved in a tight flock from one place to another, the Shelties manage the birds more easily than sheep during the learning process. In South Africa, because of their larger size, Collies are used to herd ostriches.

HANDLE WITH CARE

The Sheltie is a calm, dignified dog that does not take well to unpredictable owners. Rough and erratic training methods are not successful with Shelties. These herding dogs respond best to patient, gentle training methods and, because of their intelligence, learn quickly and eagerly.

The Shetland Sheepdog's perception of his owner's moods is remarkable. He senses all manner of human emotions and reacts accordingly. He worries with the sad owner, celebrates with the excited, happy one and so on. Actually, dogs are much like humans when it comes to emotions—they experience many of the same emotions as humans.

The ideal Sheltie owner is an active person who enjoys working with his dog, teaching him new things and going places and doing things together. He is a person who also enjoys the few minutes each day required to keep the Sheltie's coat free of mats and looking clean. A person who enjoys outdoor activities in all seasons makes a good candidate for Sheltie companionship. Because of the dog's love of master and family, a Sheltie owner must be a demonstrative person who will give love and

enjoy receiving the love of a Sheltie.

One final word about the ideal owner of a Shetland Sheepdog: Due to the dog's intelligence and love of physical activity, Shelties should be trained at an early age. They love learning and are quick to conceptualize behaviors. They willingly practice a particular behavior several times with the owner and then suddenly refuse to repeat the behavior again. From those few repetitions, they learn the desired behavior; practicing too many times proves boring to them. It's their way of saying, "You showed me what to do. I've done it. Now let's do

Shelties make ideal companions for children of all ages. It is of course essential that the children understand how to treat a dog so that mutual respect is established.

Shelties are dignified, clever dogs that adapt quickly to family life. Many Sheltie owners are amazed at how easily their dogs are trained.

Herding dogs, designed to respond to a shepherd's command and hand signal, are among the brightest of all canines. The Shetland Sheepdog, with his amenable disposition, leaps to the head of the class in all endeavors.

something else. This is boring."

The next day, the owner will be amazed to see that the dog remembers the behaviors and performs them to perfection upon hearing the commands. The Sheltie truly is one of the world's brightest canine students.

TEMPERAMENT COUNTS

Shyness, timidity, stubbornness, snappiness and bad temper are all considered major faults in Shetland Sheepdogs. They must be avoided at all costs to preserve true Sheltie temperament.

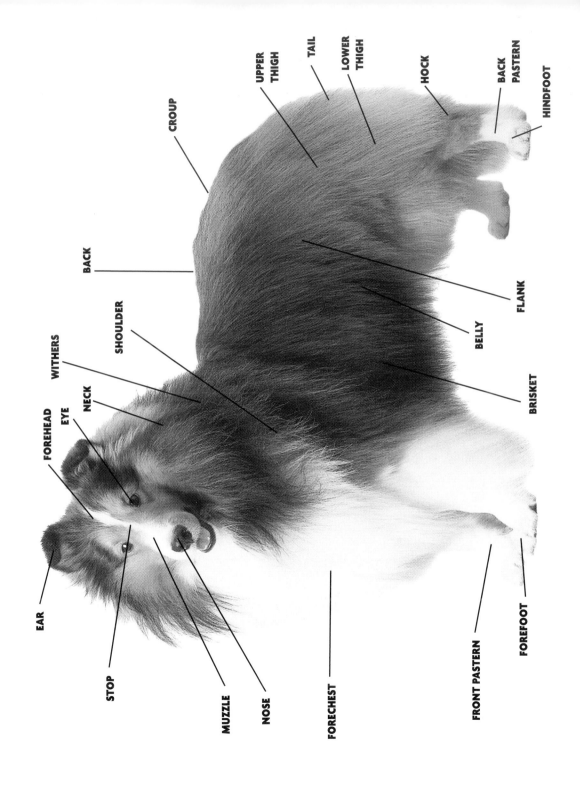

BREED STANDARD FOR THE

SHETLAND SHEEPDOG

The Shetland Sheepdog is a small, robust dog, well rounded in appearance, with no sharp angles or rigid lines when viewed from front or back. He wears a rough longhaired outer coat with a soft, dense undercoat to provide warmth in cold climates. The soft, furry undercoat must be so thick that it forces the harsh outer coat to stand up rather than lie flat against the body.

In males, the mane should be particularly abundant and impressive. Both sexes sport a large wide collar of fur around the neck, often referred to as the ruff. Overall, the Sheltie presents a symmetrical appearance, with the males being masculine and the females obviously feminine.

Coat colors are varied enough to please the most discriminating human taste. Black, blue merle and sable, ranging from golden tones to deep mahogany, are the color choices. Small amounts of white are permitted but more than 50% white is considered a fault in the show ring.

Fore and hind legs carry ample feathering down to the hock joint (ankle). Below that, the hair is short and smooth against the skin. The tail is a large full plume that the dog carries low when at rest and extended when he's working or running. Hair on the face, ears and feet should be short and smooth. For show purposes, the hair on these parts may be trimmed to present a clean look.

The dogs should weigh 25 to 30 pounds and stand about 14 inches at the shoulder. Males are slightly larger than females.

Keeping in mind that the Shetland Sheepdog should give the appearance of a Collie in miniature, any deviation from that look should be considered a serious fault in the show ring. That "Collie look" has dominated the breed for centuries—it must be fostered in every future generation. The breed standard is designed to ensure that it does.

A breed standard is a word picture of the ideal dog of a particular breed. The breed standard for the Shetland Sheepdog spells out what the dog should look and act like in detail. Features such as size, proportion, substance, head, neck, body, forequarters, hindquarters, coat, gait and temperament are all addressed in the standard.

The standard in each country varies slightly, so it's important to familiarize yourself with the standard of perfection for the Shetland Sheepdog in your country. In the US, of course, the standard used is the standard recognized by the American Kennel Club.

In addition to specific standards for desirable traits, the standard also spells out faults, both physical and temperamental, that demerit the dog if any of those faults are present. Some breed standards also include disqualifications, which forbid the dog from competing in a show if he possesses any of these egregious faults. For example, the American standard states that a short, choppy gait with stiff, jerky movements is a serious fault.

The reason that gait is considered so important in the Sheltie is that traditionally the dog must travel many miles in a day as he herds cattle or sheep. Anything

The Shetland Sheepdog should look like a Rough Collie in miniature, always symmetrical and magnificently coated.

less than lithe, smooth and graceful movement—in essence, effortless—would tire the dog so severely that he could not perform his job. Thus, he would not be considered an ideal Sheltie.

Atop the magnificently coated body is the distinctive shape of the Sheltie's head. A flat skull tapering into a blunt, wedge-shaped head from ears to black nose must not be sharp or snipy. Small ears are carried erect and the tips should fall forward.

Without that special Collie look of the head and ears, a Sheltie would hardly be called a Shetland Sheepdog. Eyes are almond-shaped and dark in color. Only the blue merles are permitted to have blue eyes.

Overall expression of the Sheltie is one of curiosity and intelligent alertness. The head is always carried proudly. The expression toward strangers should be of watchful reserve; he is never fearful or nervous.

In summary, the breed standard spells out exactly what a particular breed should and should not be. It provides the guidelines for breeders to follow in producing today's dogs and ensuring the type and quality of tomorrow's generations of pure-bred dogs.

Here we present an excerpt from the AKC breed standard, describing the positive qualities of the ideal Shetland Sheepdog.

Note the differences in type between this top-quality British dog and the American dogs in this book.

THE AMERICAN KENNEL CLUB STANDARD FOR THE SHETLAND SHEEPDOG

General Appearance: Preamble—The Shetland Sheepdog, like the Collie, traces to the Border Collie of Scotland, which, transported to the Shetland Islands and crossed with small, intelligent, longhaired breeds, was reduced to miniature proportions. Subsequently crosses were made from time to time with Collies. This breed now bears the same relationship in size and general appearance to the Rough Collie as the Shetland Pony does to some of the larger breeds of horses. Although the resemblance between the Shetland Sheepdog and the Rough Collie is marked, there are differences which may

Profile, showing correct type, balance, structure and mature coat.

be noted. The Shetland Sheepdog is a small, alert, rough-coated, longhaired working dog. He must be sound, agile and sturdy. The outline should be so symmetrical that no part appears out of proportion to the whole. Dogs should appear masculine; bitches feminine.

Size, Proportion, Substance: The Shetland Sheepdog should stand between 13 and 16 inches at the shoulder. Note: Height is determined by a line perpendicular to the ground from the top of the shoulder blades, the dog standing naturally, with forelegs parallel to line of measurement.

Head: The head should be refined and its shape, when viewed from top or side, should be a long, blunt wedge tapering slightly from ears to nose. Expression—Contours and chiseling of the head, the shape, set and use of ears, the placement, shape and color of the eyes combine to produce expression. Normally the expression should be alert, gentle, intelligent and questioning. Toward strangers the eyes should show watchfulness and reserve, but no fear. Eyes medium size with dark, almond-shaped rims, set somewhat obliquely in skull. Color must be dark, with blue or merle eyes permissible in blue merles only. Ears small and flexible, placed high, carried three-fourths erect, with tips breaking forward. When in repose the ears fold lengthwise and are thrown back into the frill. Skull and Muzzle—Top of skull should be flat, showing no prominence at nuchal crest (the top of the occiput). Cheeks should be flat and should merge smoothly into a well-rounded muzzle. Skull and muzzle should be of equal length, balance point being inner corner of eye. In profile the top line of skull should parallel the top line of muzzle, but on a higher plane due to the presence of a slight but definite stop. Jaws clean and powerful. The deep, well-developed underjaw, rounded at chin, should extend to base of nostril. Nose must be black. Lips tight. Upper and lower lips must meet and fit smoothly together all the way around. Teeth level and evenly spaced. Scissors bite.

Neck, Topline, Body: Neck should be muscular, arched, and of sufficient length to carry the head proudly. Back should be level and strongly muscled.

Chest should be deep, the brisket reaching to point of elbow. The ribs should be well sprung, but flattened at their lower half to allow free play of the foreleg and shoulder. Abdomen moderately tucked up. There should be a slight arch at the loins, and the croup should slope gradually to the rear. The hipbone (pelvis) should be set at a 30-degree angle to the spine. The tail should be sufficiently long so that when it is laid along the back edge of the hind legs the last vertebra will reach the hock

Head study, showing correct balance, type and structure.

joint. Carriage of tail at rest is straight down or in a slight upward curve. When the dog is alert the tail is normally lifted, but it should not be curved forward over the back.

Forequarters: From the withers, the shoulder blades should slope at a 45-degree angle forward and downward to the shoulder joints. The upper arm should join the shoulder blade at as nearly as possible a right angle. Elbow joint should be equidistant from the ground and from the withers. Forelegs straight viewed from all angles,

FAULTS IN PROFILE

Top: Short and heavy head, low ear carriage, short neck, upright shoulders, weak pasterns, flat feet, lacking angulation behind, tail carried too high. Bottom: Snipey muzzle, prick ears, wide front, toes out in front, low on leg, long back.

Top: Upright shoulders, lacking bone, weak pasterns, flat feet, short neck, narrow front and rear. Bottom: Semi-prick ears, loaded shoulders, wide front, long back, soft topline, low on leg, cowhocked.

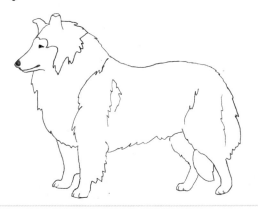

muscular and clean, and of strong bone. Pasterns very strong, sinewy and flexible. Dewclaws may be removed. Feet should be oval and compact with the toes well arched and fitting tightly together. Pads deep and tough, nails hard and strong.

Hindquarters: The thigh should be broad and muscular. The overall length of the stifle should at least equal the length of the thighbone, and preferably should slightly exceed it. Hock joint should be clean-cut, angular, sinewy, with good bone and strong ligamentation. The hock (metatarsus) should be short and straight viewed from all angles. Dewclaws should be removed. Feet as in forequarters.

Coat: The coat should be double, the outer coat consisting of long, straight, harsh hair; the undercoat short, furry, and so dense as to give the entire coat its "standoff" quality. The hair on face, tips of ears and feet should be smooth. Mane and frill should be abundant, and particularly impressive in males. The forelegs well feathered, the hind legs heavily so, but smooth below the hock joint. Hair on tail profuse.

Color: Black, blue merle, and sable (ranging from golden through mahogany); marked with varying amounts of white and/or tan.

Gait: The trotting gait of the Shetland Sheepdog should denote effortless speed and smoothness. The drive should be from the rear, true and straight, dependent upon correct angulation, musculation, and ligamentation of the entire hindquarter, thus allowing the dog to reach well under his body with his hind foot and propel himself forward. Viewed from the front, both forelegs and hindlegs should move forward almost perpendicular to ground at the walk, slanting a little inward at a slow trot, until at a swift trot the feet are brought so far inward toward center line of body that the tracks left show two parallel lines of footprints actually touching a center line at their inner edges.

Temperament: Intensely loyal, affectionate, and responsive to his owner. However, he may be reserved toward strangers but not to the point of showing fear or cringing in the ring.

Disqualifications:
Heights below or above the desired size range, i.e., 13-16 inches.
Brindle color.

SHETLAND SHEEPDOG

You should acquire your Sheltie puppy from a good breeder with an established reputation. Puppies at just four weeks of age are beginning to display their individual personalities.

WHERE TO BEGIN?

As with all other breeds of dog, there are many hereditary problems to consider when choosing a Sheltie puppy. If a breeder ignores your questions about certifying his breeding stock from congenital diseases, no matter his reasoning, find another breeder. Every reputable breeder is concerned about his dogs' health and genetic contributions to future generations. He makes every effort to be well informed about the breed's health problems and veterinary science's role in curing and/or preventing such problems in the future. A

good breeder will be eager to explain health concerns to you and share the knowledge he has in regards to his breeding stock. He will also be anxious to share with you the name and address of his dogs' vet, with whom you may want to speak concerning the parents of the litter.

In addition to major health concerns, there are other considerations to be aware of when acquiring a puppy. Here are some things to think about:

1. When you arrive at the breeder's kennel, look around the place before you even look at the litter. Is it clean? Is there a place for the puppies to play, eat and sleep, or are they crowded in a small space on newspaper?

TEMPERAMENT COUNTS

Your selection of a good puppy can be determined by your needs. A show potential or a good pet? It is your choice. Every puppy, however, should be of good temperament. Although show-quality puppies are bred and raised with emphasis on physical conformation, responsible breeders strive for equally good temperament. Do not buy from a breeder who concentrates solely on physical beauty at the expense of personality.

2. When you first see the litter, do the puppies come running to you in friendly anticipation or do they run away and cringe in fear?

3. What about the parents? Are they well cared for and clean? Are they friendly, standoffish or aggressive? You should know that the temperament of the parents probably indicates what the puppies will be like when they grow up. By all means, puppies should be especially friendly and happy, with little or no sense of protectiveness at early ages.

4. No doubt you will have an opportunity to observe some puppy feces. Is the stool well formed and solid? Loose, runny stools are a cause for concern and should be checked by a vet, who will be looking for the cause such as worms, infection, bacterial infestations, etc.

5. How do the puppies interact with the breeder? They should not show fear but instead be happy to see him and anxious for attention. If you observe one particular puppy sitting off in a corner by himself, that puppy is not a good candidate for you; he will probably grow up to be shy, perhaps even a fear-biter.

6. As your eyes (and your heart) gravitate toward one particular puppy, take a careful look at him. Is he clean? Does he smell good with sweet puppy breath?

Breeding from sound, healthy dogs produces sound, healthy pups. The pups then get the best start in life from their mother's milk.

Are his eyes bright and shiny, his nose cool and not running? Is he coughing? Does he have fleas or any other parasites?

7. Check out the sex of the puppies that you are interested in. Before you began your search, you should have decided which sex was best for you and your family. Keep in mind that male dogs should be neutered and female dogs spayed at the appropriate age unless they are destined for breeding or showing. Discuss

TIME TO GO HOME
Breeders rarely release puppies until they are eight to ten weeks of age. This is an acceptable age for most breeds of dog, excepting toy breeds, which are not released until around 12 weeks, given their petite sizes. If a breeder has a puppy that is 12 weeks of age or older, he is likely well social-ized and house-trained. Be sure that he is otherwise healthy before decid-ing to take him home.

the proper age and the advantages of neutering with your veterinarian.

8. Finally, does the breeder have the proper registration papers for the American Kennel Club to go with the puppy of your choice? The breeder should also provide you with a feeding schedule and whatever else you need to make the puppy's transition from birth home to your home as easy and stress-free as possible. A pedigree is also a necessary document to get with your puppy. Tracing the history of your puppy's family, the pedigree tells you the registered names of parents, grandparents and great-grandparents on both the puppy's sire's and dam's sides. It also documents any degrees and/or titles those relatives might have earned, which can help you understand the physical conformation and/or training accomplishments of your pup's relatives.

If you have intentions for your new charge to herd sheep, there are many more considerations. The parents of a future working dog should have excellent qualifications, including actual work experience as well as working titles in their pedigrees. Working Shelties are less common than, say, working Border Collies, but it is not impossible to acquire such a dog. By and large, the breed still maintains its working instincts. Look in farming newspapers and stock-dog journals to find the Shetland Sheepdogs that are trained and bred for working purposes.

Breeders commonly allow visitors to see their litters by around the fifth or sixth week, and puppies leave for their new homes between the eighth and tenth week. Breeders who permit their puppies to leave early are more interested in your money than their puppies' well-being. Puppies need to learn the rules of the trade from their dams, and most dams continue teaching the pups manners and dos and don'ts

PUPPY APPEARANCE
Your puppy should have a well-fed appearance but not a distended abdomen, which may indicate worms or incorrect feeding, or both. The body should be firm, with a solid feel. The skin of the abdomen should be pale pink and clean, without signs of scratching or rash. Check the hind legs to make certain that dewclaws were removed; this is done at a few days old.

All other considerations are insignificant unless the puppy you select is healthy, alert and sound.

until around the eighth week. Breeders spend significant amounts of time with the Shetland Sheepdog toddlers so that they are able to interact with the "other species," i.e., humans. Given the long history that dogs and humans have, bonding between the two species is natural but must be nurtured. A well-bred, well-socialized Shetland Sheepdog pup wants nothing more than to be near you and please you.

YOUR SCHEDULE...

If you lead an erratic, unpredictable life, with daily or weekly changes in your work requirements, consider the problems of owning a puppy. The new puppy has to be fed regularly, socialized (loved, petted, handled, introduced to other people) and, most importantly, allowed to go outdoors for house-training. As the dog gets older, he can be more tolerant of deviations in his feeding and relief schedule.

The warmth of his mother and littermates provides a secure, nurturing environment for the pup in his early weeks of life.

COMMITMENT OF OWNERSHIP

After considering all of these factors, you have most likely already made some very important decisions about selecting your puppy. You have chosen the Shetland Sheepdog, which means that you have decided which characteristics you want in a dog and what type of dog will best fit into your family and lifestyle. If you have selected a breeder, you have gone a step

BOY OR GIRL?

An important consideration to be discussed is the sex of your puppy. For a family companion, a bitch may be the better choice, considering the female's inbred concern for all young creatures and her accompanying tolerance and patience. It is always advisable to spay a pet bitch or neuter a pet dog, which may guarantee your Sheltie a longer life.

further—you have done your research and found a responsible, conscientious person who breeds quality Shetland Sheepdogs and who should be a reliable source of help as you and your puppy adjust to life together. If you have observed a litter in action, you have obtained a firsthand look at the dynamics of a puppy "pack" and, thus, you should have learned about each pup's individual personality—perhaps you have even found one that particularly appeals to you.

However, even if you have not yet found the Shetland Sheepdog puppy of your dreams, observing pups will help you learn to recognize certain behavior and to determine what a pup's behavior indicates about his temperament. You will be able to pick out which pups are the leaders, which ones are less outgoing, which ones are confident, which ones are shy, playful, friendly, aggressive, etc. Equally as important, you will learn to recognize what a healthy pup should look and act like. All of these things will help you in your search, and when you find the Shetland Sheepdog that was meant for you, you will know it!

Researching the breed, selecting a responsible breeder and observing as many pups as possible are all important steps on the way to dog ownership. It may seem like a lot of effort...and you

Gentle handling and human interaction from an early age helps puppies grow up to be well adjusted.

have not even brought the pup home yet! Remember, though, you cannot be too careful when it comes to deciding on the type of dog you want and finding out about your prospective pup's background. Buying a puppy is not—or *should* not be—just another whimsical purchase. This is one instance in which you actually do get to choose your own family! You may be thinking that buying a puppy should be fun—it should not be so serious and so much work. Keep in mind that your puppy is not a cuddly stuffed toy or decorative lawn ornament, but a creature that will become a real member of your family. You will come to realize that, while buying a puppy is a pleasurable and exciting endeavor, it is not something to be taken lightly. Relax…the fun will start when the pup comes home!

Always keep in mind that a puppy is nothing more than a baby in a furry disguise…a baby who is virtually helpless in a human world and who trusts his owner for fulfillment of his basic needs for survival. In addition to food, water and shelter, your pup needs care, protection, guidance and love. If you are not prepared to commit to this, then you are not prepared to own a dog.

"Wait a minute," you say. "How hard could this be? All of

Breeders introduce toys to the litter as a part of socialization. Be advised not to offer your puppy toys designed for humans. Dog toys are a specialty that must be obtained from a pet shop or supply store.

PEDIGREE VS. REGISTRATION CERTIFICATE

Too often new owners are confused between these two important documents. Your puppy's pedigree, essentially a family tree, is a written record of a dog's genealogy of three generations or more. The pedigree will show you the names as well as performance titles of all the dogs in your pup's background. Your breeder must provide you with a registration application, with his part properly filled out. You must complete the application and send it to the AKC with the proper fee. Every puppy must come from a litter that has been AKC-registered by the breeder, born in the USA and from a sire and dam that are also registered with the AKC.

The seller must provide you with complete records to identify the puppy. The AKC requires that the seller provide the buyer with the following: breed; sex, color and markings; date of birth; litter number (when available); names and registration numbers of the parents; breeder's name; and date sold or delivered.

to do before bringing your Shetland Sheepdog puppy home. You will also have to prepare your home and family for the new addition. Much as you would prepare a nursery for a newborn baby, you will need to designate a place in your home that will be the puppy's own. How you prepare your home will depend on how much freedom the dog will be allowed. Whatever you decide, you must ensure that he

Oftentimes an owner can choose a puppy before the pup is old enough to leave the breeder. The breeder will "hold" the puppy until the pup is a proper age to go to his new home.

my neighbors own dogs and they seem to be doing just fine. Why should I have to worry about all of this?" Well, you should not worry about it; in fact, you will probably find that once your Shetland Sheepdog pup gets used to his new home, he will fall into his place in the family quite naturally. But it never hurts to emphasize the commitment of dog ownership. With some time and patience, it is really not too difficult to raise a curious and exuberant Shetland Sheepdog pup to be a well-adjusted and well-mannered adult dog—a dog that could be your most loyal friend.

PREPARING PUPPY'S PLACE IN YOUR HOME

Researching your breed and finding a breeder are only two aspects of the "homework" you will have

ARE YOU PREPARED?

Unfortunately, when a puppy is bought by someone who does not take into consideration the time and attention that dog ownership requires, it is the puppy who suffers when he is either abandoned or placed in a shelter by a frustrated owner. So all of the "homework" you do in preparation for your pup's arrival will benefit you both. The more informed you are, the more you will know what to expect and the better equipped you will be to handle the ups and downs of raising a puppy. Hopefully, everyone in the household is willing to do his part in raising and caring for the pup. The anticipation of owning a dog often brings a lot of promises from excited family members: "I will walk him every day," "I will feed him," "I will house-train him," etc., but these things take time and effort, and promises can easily be forgotten once the novelty of the new pet has worn off.

Your Sheltie puppy will adapt quickly to his new environment and make himself feel at home. Establish the house rules immediately and be consistent. Will he or will he not be allowed on the furniture?

has a place that he can "call his own."

When you bring your new puppy into your home, you are bringing him into what will become his home as well. Obviously, you did not buy a puppy so that he could take control of your

house, but in order for a puppy to grow into a stable, well-adjusted dog, he has to feel comfortable in his surroundings. Remember, he is leaving the warmth and security of his mother and littermates, as well as the familiarity of the only place he has ever known, so it is important to make his transition as easy as possible. By preparing a place in your home for the puppy, you are making him feel as welcome as possible in a strange new place. It should not take him long to get used to it, but the sudden shock of being transplanted is somewhat traumatic for a young pup. Imagine how a small child would feel in the same situation—that is how your puppy must be feeling. It is up to you to reassure him and to let him know, "Little fuzzball, you are going to like it here!"

WHAT YOU SHOULD BUY

CRATE
To someone unfamiliar with the use of crates in dog training, it may seem like punishment to shut a dog in a crate, but this is not the case at all. Most professional breeders and trainers recommend the dog crate as a preferred tool for show puppies and pet puppies alike. Crates are not cruel—crates have many humane and highly effective uses in dog care and training. For example, crate training is a very popular and very

PET INSURANCE
Just like you can insure your car, your house and your own health, you likewise can insure your dog's health. Investigate a pet insurance policy by talking to your vet. Depending on the age of your dog, the breed and the kind of coverage you desire, your policy can be very affordable. Most policies cover accidental injuries, poisoning and thousands of medical problems and illnesses, including cancers. Some carriers also offer routine care and immunization coverage.

successful housebreaking method. A crate can keep your dog safe during travel and, perhaps most importantly, a crate provides your dog with a place of his own in your home.

Crate training should be among an owner's first considerations with a new Sheltie. Teaching the dog or puppy to enjoy using his crate offers protection from all manner of injuries to the dog to say nothing of keeping your home safe from puppy destruction. Having his own crate provides security for the dog and gives him a safe place to stay while you are out of the home and unable to supervise him. A common complaint for pet owners is that the dog literally destroys the house whenever he is left alone. This is called isolation frustration, and it occurs when the dog is given too much freedom without human supervision. The solution to the problem is offering a place of security to the dog so that he has no need to be anxious about being alone. This little den is the answer.

Many dogs sleep in their crates overnight. When lined with soft bedding and a favorite toy, a crate becomes a cozy pseudo-den for your dog. Like his ancestors, he too will seek out the comfort and retreat of a den—you are providing him with something a little more luxurious than what his early ancestors enjoyed.

CRATE-TRAINING TIPS

During crate training, you should partition off the section of the crate in which the pup stays. If he is given too big an area, this will hinder your training efforts. Crate training is based on the fact that a dog does not like to soil his sleeping quarters, so it is ineffective to keep a pup in a crate that is so big that he can eliminate in one end and get far enough away from it to sleep. Also, you want to make the crate den-like for the pup. Blankets and a favorite toy will make the crate cozy for the small pup; as he grows, you may want to evict some of his "roommates" to make more room. It will take some coaxing at first, but be patient. Given some time to get used to it, your Sheltie will adapt to his new home-within-a-home quite nicely.

As far as purchasing a crate, the type that you buy is up to you. It will most likely be one of the two most popular types: wire or

fiberglass. There are advantages and disadvantages to each type. For example, a wire crate is more open, allowing the air to flow through and affording the dog a view of what is going on around him, while a fiberglass crate is sturdier. Both can double as travel crates, providing protection for the dog. The size of the crate is another thing to consider. Since Shelties are smallish dogs, a medium-size crate will be necessary for a full-grown Shetland Sheepdog, who stands approximately 14 inches high.

GATES

While on the subject of housing, let's talk about baby gates. These low dividers are primarily manufactured for use in keeping children confined to certain areas of the home. However, they are equally effective in confining dogs to certain rooms. When you're housebreaking a puppy, you will be more successful if he's limited to small areas where you can keep an eye on him until he's completely reliable regarding his house-training (usually until about six months of age).

BEDDING

A crate pad in the dog's crate will help the dog feel more at home, and you may also like to put in a small blanket. This will take the place of the leaves, twigs, etc., that the pup would use in the

FINANCIAL RESPONSIBILITY

Grooming tools, collars, leashes, a crate, a dog bed and, of course, toys will be expenses to you when you first obtain your pup, and the cost will continue throughout your dog's lifetime. If your puppy damages or destroys your possessions (as most puppies surely will!) or something belonging to a neighbor, you can calculate additional expense. There is also flea and pest control, which every dog owner faces more than once. You must be able to handle the financial responsibility of owning a dog.

littermates, and while a blanket is not the same as a warm, breathing body, it still provides heat and something with which to snuggle. You will want to wash your pup's blanket frequently in case he has a potty accident in his crate, and replace or remove anything that becomes ragged and starts to fall apart.

Toys
Toys are a must for dogs of all ages, especially for curious playful pups. Puppies are the "children" of the dog world, and what

wild to make a den; the pup can make his own "burrow" in the crate. Although your pup is far removed from his den-making ancestors, the denning instinct is still a part of his genetic makeup. Second, until you bring your pup home, he has been sleeping amid the warmth of his mother and

Show dogs absolutely must be crate trained. Crates are ideal for travel to and from the shows and for accommodation while the Sheltie awaits his turn in the ring.

Your local pet shop will have various sizes, colors and types of dog crates available for your selection.

PHOTO COURTESY OF DOSKOCIL.

QUALITY FOOD
The cost of food must be mentioned. All dogs need a good-quality food with an adequate supply of protein to develop their bones and muscles properly. Most dogs are not picky eaters but, unless fed properly, can quickly succumb to skin problems.

A wire pen gives the puppies sunshine and exercise while confined outdoors. Breeders and exhibitors commonly use these at shows, as they are easily collapsed for transport.

chewing is a physical need for pups as they are teething, and everything looks appetizing! The full range of your possessions—from old dishcloth to Oriental rug—are fair game in the eyes of a teething pup. Puppies are not all that discerning when it comes to finding something to literally "sink their teeth into"—everything tastes great!

Shetland Sheepdog puppies are fairly aggressive chewers and only the hardest, strongest toys should be offered to them. Breeders advise owners to resist stuffed toys, because they can become de-stuffed in no time. The overly excited pup may ingest the stuffing, which is neither nutritious nor digestible.

child does not love toys? Chew toys provide enjoyment to both dog and owner—your dog will enjoy playing with his favorite toys, while you will enjoy the fact that they distract him from your expensive shoes and leather sofa. Puppies love to chew; in fact,

Be certain that your Sheltie's outdoor accommodations are secure. Gates must close completely and lock for the safety of your Shelties.

PUPPY PROBLEMS

The majority of problems that are commonly seen in young pups will disappear as your dog gets older. However, how you deal with problems when he is young will determine how he reacts to discipline as an adult dog. It is important to establish who is boss (hopefully it will be you!) right away when you are first bonding with your dog. This bond will set the tone for the rest of your life together

which have a tendency to splinter into sharp, dangerous pieces. Also be careful of rawhide, which can turn into pieces that are easy to swallow or into a mushy mess on your carpet.

LEASH

A nylon leash is probably the best option, as it is the most resistant to puppy teeth should your pup take a liking to chewing on his leash. Of course, this is a habit that should be nipped in the bud, but, if your pup likes to chew on his leash, he has a very slim chance of being able to chew through the strong nylon. Nylon leashes are also lightweight, which is good for a young Shetland Sheepdog who is just getting used to the idea of walking on a leash. For everyday walking and safety purposes, the nylon leash is a good choice.

A small gate is no match for a curious Sheltie pup! Make sure the gate you select is tall enough to keep your Sheltie safely confined.

Similarly, squeaky toys are quite popular, but must be avoided for the Shetland Sheepdog. Perhaps a squeaky toy can be used as an aid in training, but not for free play. If a pup "disembowels" one of these, the small plastic squeaker inside can be dangerous if swallowed. Monitor the condition of all your pup's toys carefully and get rid of any that have been chewed to the point of becoming potentially dangerous.

Be careful of natural bones,

THE INVISIBLE FENCE

The electrical fencing system, which forms an invisible fence, works on a battery-operated collar that shocks the dog if it gets too close to the buried (or elevated) wire. There are some people who think very highly of this system of controlling a dog's wandering. Keep in mind that the collar has batteries. For safety's sake, replace the batteries every month with the best-quality batteries available.

Tug toys are extremely popular with Shelties. Only use ropes made especially for dogs and with non-toxic dyes.

TOYS, TOYS, TOYS!

With a big variety of dog toys available, and so many that look like they would be a lot of fun for a dog, be careful in your selection. It is amazing what a set of puppy teeth can do to an innocent-looking toy; so, obviously, safety is a major consideration. Be sure to choose the most durable products that you can find. Hard nylon bones and toys are a safe bet, and many of them are offered in different scents and flavors that will be sure to capture your dog's attention. It is always fun to play a game of fetch with your dog, and there are balls and flying discs that are specially made to withstand dog teeth.

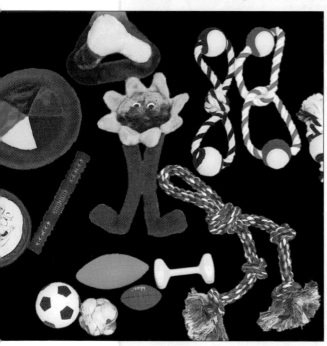

As your pup grows up and gets used to walking on the leash, and can do it politely, you may want to purchase a flexible leash. These leashes allow you to extend the length to give the dog a broader area to explore or to shorten the length to keep the dog close to you.

COLLAR

Your pup should get used to wearing a collar all the time since you will want to attach his ID tags to it. Also, you have to attach the leash to something! A lightweight nylon collar is a good choice; make sure that it fits snugly enough so that the pup cannot wriggle out of it, but is loose enough so that it will not be uncomfortably tight around the pup's neck. You should be able to fit a finger between the pup and the collar. It may take some time for your pup to get used to wearing the collar, but soon he will not even notice that it is there. The snap collars are handy and easy to use. Buckle collars are also suitable, but be careful not to entangle the dog's fur in the collar. A chain collar is not necessary for any puppy or adult Shelties. They are more than willing to stay by your side and not pull when you walk together. It's truly the Sheltie's nature to heel.

FOOD AND WATER BOWLS

Your pup will need two bowls, one for food and one for water. You may want two sets of bowls, one for inside and one for outside, depending on where the dog will be fed and where he will be spending his time. Stainless steel or sturdy plastic bowls are popular choices. Plastic bowls are more chewable. Dogs tend not to chew on the steel variety, which can be sterilized. It is important to buy sturdy bowls

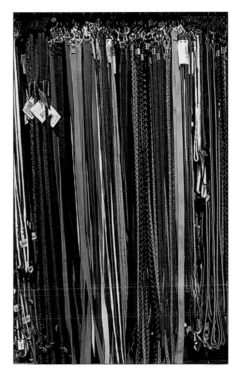

Pet shops usually stock large quantities of dog leashes. Select the leash that suits your taste and needs. The Sheltie does not require a very heavy leash.

since anything is in danger of being chewed by puppy teeth and you do not want your dog to be constantly chewing apart his bowl (for his safety and for your wallet!).

CLEANING SUPPLIES

Until a pup is house-trained, you will be doing a lot of cleaning. Accidents will occur, which is okay in the beginning because the puppy does not know any better. All you can do is be prepared to clean up any accidents. Old rags, paper towels, newspapers and a safe disinfectant are good to have on hand.

IN DUE TIME

It will take at least two weeks for your puppy to become accustomed to his new surroundings. Give him lots of love, attention, handling, frequent opportunities to relieve himself, a diet he likes to eat and a place he can call his own.

CHOOSE AN APPROPRIATE COLLAR

The **BUCKLE COLLAR** is the standard collar used for everyday purposes. Be sure that you adjust the buckle on growing puppies. Check it every day. It can become too tight overnight! These collars can be made of leather or nylon. Attach your dog's identification tags to this collar.

The **CHOKE COLLAR** is designed for training. It is constructed of highly polished steel so that it slides easily through the stainless steel loop. The idea is that the dog controls the pressure around his neck and he will stop pulling if the collar becomes uncomfortable. It is neither necessary nor recommended for the Shetland Sheepdog.

The **HALTER** is for a trained dog that has to be restrained to prevent running away, chasing a cat and the like. Considered the most humane of all collars, it is frequently used on smaller dogs on which collars are not comfortable.

BEYOND THE BASICS

The items previously discussed are the bare necessities. You will find out what else you need as you go along—grooming supplies, flea/tick protection, etc. These things will vary depending on your situation but it is important that you have everything you need to feed and make your Shetland Sheepdog comfortable in his first few days at home.

PUPPY-PROOFING YOUR HOME

Aside from making sure that your Shetland Sheepdog will be comfortable in your home, you also have to make sure that your home is safe for your Shetland Sheepdog. This means taking precautions that your pup will not get into anything he should not get into and that there is nothing within his reach that may harm him should he sniff it, chew it, inspect it, etc. This probably seems obvious since, while you are primarily concerned with your pup's safety, at the same time you do not want your belongings to be ruined. Breakables should be placed out of reach if your dog is to have full run of the house. If he is to be limited to certain places within the house, keep any potentially dangerous items in the "off-limits" areas. An electrical wire can pose a danger should the puppy decide to taste it—and who is going to convince

Select durable, easily cleaned bowls for your Sheltie.

Stainless steel or heavy plastic bowls are two of the most popular types for dogs.

a pup that it would not make a great chew toy? Wires should be fastened tightly against the wall, out of the Sheltie's reach. If your dog is going to spend time in a crate, make sure that there is nothing near his crate that he can reach if he sticks his curious little nose or paws through the openings. Just as you would with

Special equipment is available to make cleaning up after your dog in the yard a lot easier.

a child, keep all household cleaners and chemicals where the pup cannot get to them.

It is also important to make sure that the outside of your home is safe. Of course your puppy should never be unsupervised, but a pup let loose in the yard will want to run and explore, and he should be granted that freedom. Do not let a fence give you a false sense of security; you would be surprised how crafty (and persistent) a dog can be in figuring out how to dig under and squeeze his way through small holes, or to jump or climb over a fence. The remedy is to make the fence high enough so that it really is impossible for your dog to get over it (6 feet should suffice), and well embedded into the ground. Be sure to repair or secure any gaps in the fence. Check the fence peri-

THE RIDE HOME

Taking your dog from the breeder to your home in a car can be a very uncomfortable experience for both of you. The puppy will have been taken from his warm, friendly, safe environment and brought into a strange new environment—an environment that moves! Be prepared for loose bowels, urination, crying, whining and even fear biting. With proper love and encouragement when you arrive home, the stress of the trip should quickly disappear.

Although your pup may enjoy them, children's toys are not made to withstand dog teeth and may have small parts that can break off easily. Fortunately, there are many equally fun toys made for dogs, with their safety in mind, and these are what should be offered to your Sheltie.

odically to ensure that it is in good shape and make repairs as needed; a very determined pup may return to the same spot to "work on it" until he is able to get through.

FIRST TRIP TO THE VET

You have picked out your puppy, and your home and family are ready. Now all you have to do is

SKULL & CROSSBONES

Thoroughly puppy-proof your house before bringing your puppy home. Never use cockroach or rodent poisons or plant fertilizers in any area accessible to the puppy. Avoid the use of toilet cleaners. Most dogs are born with "toilet-bowl sonar" and will take a drink if the lid is left open. Also keep the trash secured and out of reach.

Shetland Sheepdog puppies live to play. Whether it's chasing a ball, fetching a flying disc or "herding" their owner's children, puppies look forward to lots of daily fun.

TOXIC PLANTS

Many plants can be toxic to dogs. If you see your dog carrying a piece of vegetation in his mouth, approach him in a quiet, disinterested manner, avoid eye contact, pet him and gradually remove the plant from his mouth. Alternatively, offer him a treat and maybe he'll drop the plant on his own accord. Be sure no toxic plants are growing in your own garden.

collect your Shetland Sheepdog from the breeder and the fun begins, right? Well…not so fast. Something else you need to prepare is your pup's first trip to the veterinarian. Perhaps the breeder can recommend someone in the area who works with many Shetland Sheepdogs, or maybe you know some other Shetland Sheepdog owners who can suggest a good vet. Either way, you should have an appointment arranged for your pup before you pick him up and plan on taking him for an examination before bringing him home.

The pup's first visit will consist of an overall examination to make sure that the pup does not have any problems that are not apparent to you. The veterinarian will also set up a schedule for the pup's vaccinations; the breeder will inform you of which ones the pup has already received and the vet can continue from there.

INTRODUCTION TO THE FAMILY

Everyone in the house will be excited about the puppy's coming home and will want to pet him and play with him, but it is best to make the introductions low-key so as not to overwhelm the puppy. He is apprehensive already. It is the first time he has been separated from his mother and the breeder, and the ride to your home is likely the first time he has been in a car. The last thing you want to do is smother him, as this will only frighten him further. This is not to say that human contact is not extremely necessary at this stage, because this is the time when a connection between the pup and his human family is formed. Gentle petting and soothing words should help console him, as well as just putting him down and letting him explore on his own (under your watchful eye, of course).

The pup may approach the family members or may busy himself with exploring for a while. Gradually, each person should spend some time with the pup, one at a time, crouching down to get as close to the pup's level as possible and letting him sniff their hands and petting him gently. He definitely needs human attention and he needs to be touched—this is how to form an immediate bond. Just remem-

ber that the pup is experiencing a lot of things for the first time, at the same time. There are new people, new noises, new smells and new things to investigate, so be gentle, be affectionate and be as comforting as you can be.

Keep the "getting to know you" sessions low-key and always supervise introductions between children and the Sheltie.

CHEMICAL TOXINS

Scour your garage for potential puppy dangers. Remove weed killers, pesticides and antifreeze materials. Antifreeze is highly toxic and just a few drops can kill a puppy or an adult dog. The sweet taste attracts the animal, who will quickly consume it from the floor or pavement.

YOUR PUP'S FIRST NIGHT HOME

You have traveled home with your new charge safely in his crate or on a friend's lap. He's been to the vet for a thorough checkup; he's been weighed, his papers examined; perhaps he's even been vaccinated and wormed as well. He's met the family and licked the whole family, including the excited children and the less-than-happy cat. He's explored his area, his new bed, the yard and anywhere else he's been permitted. He's eaten his first meal at home and relieved himself in the proper place. He's heard lots of new sounds, smelled new friends and seen more of the outside world than ever before.

That was just the first day! He's worn out and ready for bed…or so you think!

It's puppy's first night and you are ready to say "Good night"—keep in mind that this is puppy's first night ever to be sleeping alone. His dam and littermates are no longer at paw's length and he's a bit scared, cold and lonely. Be reassuring to your new family member, but this is not the time to spoil him and give in to his inevitable whining.

Puppies whine. They whine to let others know where they are and hopefully to get company out of it. Place your pup in his new bed or crate in his room and close the crate door. Mercifully, he may fall asleep without a peep. When the inevitable occurs, ignore the whining; he is fine. Be strong and keep his interest in mind. Do not allow your heart to become guilty and visit the pup. He will fall asleep.

Many breeders recommend placing a piece of bedding from the pup's former home in his new bed so that he recognizes the scent of his littermates. Others still advise placing a hot water bottle in his bed for warmth. This latter may be a good idea provided the pup doesn't attempt to suckle—he'll get good and wet and may not fall asleep so fast.

Puppy's first night can be somewhat stressful for the pup and his new family. Remember that you are setting the tone of nighttime at your house. Unless you want to play with your pup every night at 10 p.m., midnight and 2 a.m., don't initiate the habit. Your family will thank you, and soon so will your pup!

Choose a cozy but safe place for the Sheltie puppy to stay in your home. Keep the pup away from anything that can cause him harm.

PREVENTING PUPPY PROBLEMS

SOCIALIZATION

Now that you have done all of the preparatory work and have helped your pup get accustomed to his new home and family, it is about time for you to have some fun! Socializing your Shetland Sheepdog pup gives you the opportunity to show off your new friend,

and your pup gets to reap the benefits of being an adorable furry creature that people will want to pet and, in general, think is absolutely precious!

Besides getting to know his new family, your puppy should be exposed to other people, animals and situations, but of course he must not come into close contact with dogs you don't know well until his course of injections is fully complete. Socialization will help him become well adjusted as he grows up and less prone to being timid or fearful of the new things he will encounter. Your pup's socialization began at the breeder's, but now it is your responsibility to continue it. The socialization he receives up until

Each member of the household should spend some time with the new arrival, including the children. Since children tend to be excited about meeting the puppy, adults should supervise the proceedings.

The move from his dam and littermates to your home is a big transition for a small pup, but your Sheltie will become part of the family in no time!

> ### STRESS-FREE
> Some experts in canine health advise that stress during a dog's early years of development can compromise and weaken his immune system, and may trigger the potential for a shortened life. They emphasize the need for happy and stress-free growing-up years.

the age of 12 weeks is the most critical, as this is the time when he forms his impressions of the outside world. Be especially careful during the eight-to-ten-week-old period, also known as the fear period. The interaction he receives during this time should be gentle and reassuring. Lack of socialization can manifest itself in fear and aggression as the dog grows up. He needs lots of human contact, affection, handling and exposure to other animals.

Once your pup has received his necessary vaccinations, feel free to take him out and about (on his leash, of course). Walk him around the neighborhood, take him on your daily errands, let people pet him, let him meet other dogs and pets, etc. Puppies do not have to try to make friends; there will be no shortage of people who will want to introduce themselves. Just make sure that you carefully supervise

PUP MEETS WORLD
Thorough socialization includes not only meeting new people but also being introduced to new experiences such as riding in the car, having his coat brushed, hearing the television, walking in a crowd—the list is endless. The more your pup experiences, and the more positive the experiences are, the less of a shock and the less frightening it will be for your pup to encounter new things.

each meeting. If the neighborhood children want to say hello, for example, that is great—children and pups most often make great companions. However, sometimes an excited child can unintentionally handle a pup too roughly, or an overzealous pup can playfully nip a little too hard. You want to make socialization experiences positive ones. What a pup learns during this very formative stage will impact his attitude toward future encounters. You want your dog to be comfortable around everyone. A pup that has a bad experience with a child may grow up to be a dog that is shy around or aggressive toward children.

CONSISTENCY IN TRAINING
Dogs, being pack animals, naturally need a leader, or else they try to establish dominance in their packs. When you bring a dog into your family, the choice of who becomes the leader and who becomes the "pack" is entirely up to you! Your pup's intuitive quest for dominance, coupled with the fact that it is nearly impossible to look at an adorable Shetland Sheepdog pup, with his "puppy-dog" eyes and his furry face, and not cave in, give the pup almost an unfair advantage in getting the upper hand! A pup will definitely test the waters to see what he can and cannot do. Do not give in to those pleading eyes—stand your ground when it comes to disci-

plining the pup and make sure that all family members do the same. It will only confuse the pup when Mother tells him to get off the couch when he is used to sitting up there with Father to watch the nightly news. Avoid discrepancies by having all members of the household decide on the rules before the pup even comes home…and be consistent in enforcing them! Early training shapes the dog's personality, so you cannot be unclear in what you expect.

COMMON PUPPY PROBLEMS

The best way to prevent puppy problems is to be proactive in stopping an undesirable behavior as soon as it starts. The old saying "You can't teach an old dog new tricks" does not necessarily hold true, but it is true that it *is* much

All puppies need a leader, and these Sheltie babies seem to be content in following their young friend.

easier to discourage bad behavior in a young developing pup than to wait until the pup's bad behavior becomes the adult dog's bad habit. There are some problems that are especially prevalent in puppies as they develop.

NIPPING

Shelties need to learn to inhibit their bite reflex and never use their teeth on people, forbidden objects and other animals in play. Whenever you play with your puppy, you make the rules. This becomes an important message to your puppy in teaching him that you are the pack leader and control everything he does in life. Once your dog accepts you as his leader, your relationship with him is cemented for life!

MANNERS MATTER

During the socialization process, a puppy should meet people, experience different environments and definitely be exposed to other canines. Through playing and interacting with other dogs, your puppy will learn lessons, ranging from controlling the pressure of his jaws by biting his littermates to the inner-workings of the canine pack that he will apply to his human relationships for the rest of his life. That is why removing a puppy from the litter too early (before eight weeks) can be detrimental to the pup's development.

And in Shelties, the genetic factor for a permanent attachment to a master is so strong that he's literally born looking for a leader.

Nipping must be discouraged immediately and consistently with a firm "No!" (or whatever number of firm "Nos" it takes for him to understand that you mean business). Then replace your finger with an appropriate chew toy. While this behavior is merely annoying when the dog is young, it can become dangerous as your Shetland Sheepdog's adult teeth grow in and his jaws develop, and he continues to think it is okay to gnaw on human appendages. Realize that your Sheltie does not mean any harm with a friendly nip, and his herding instincts and nipping

CHEWING TIPS

Chewing goes hand in hand with nipping in the sense that a teething puppy is always looking for a way to soothe his aching gums. In this case, instead of chewing on you, he may have taken a liking to your favorite shoe or something else that he should not be chewing. Again, realize that this is a normal canine behavior that does not need to be discouraged, only redirected. Your pup just needs to be taught what is acceptable to chew on and what is off-limits. Consistently tell him "No!" when you catch him chewing on something forbidden and give him a chew toy.

Conversely, praise him when you catch him chewing on something appropriate. In this way, you are discouraging the inappropriate behavior and reinforcing the desired behavior. The puppy's chewing should stop after his adult teeth have come in, but an adult dog continues to chew for various reasons—perhaps because he is bored, needs to relieve tension or just likes to chew. That is why it is important to redirect his chewing when he is still young.

may go paw in paw. Many herding dogs move their charges by nipping at their heels—your talented Sheltie may try this mechanism on the family cat, children or even you.

CRYING/WHINING

Your pup will often cry, whine, whimper, howl or make some type of commotion when he is left alone. This is basically his way of calling out for attention to make sure that you know he is there and that you have not forgotten about him. He feels insecure when he is left alone, when you are out of the house and he is in his crate or when you are in another part of the house and he cannot see you. The noise he is making is an expression of the anxiety he feels at being alone, so he needs to be taught that being alone is okay. You are not actually training the dog to stop making noise, you are training him to feel comfortable when he is alone and thus removing the need for him to make the noise. This is where the crate with cozy bedding and a toy comes in handy. You want to know that he is safe when you are not there to supervise, and you know that he will be safe in his crate rather than roaming freely about the house. In order for the pup to stay in his crate without making a fuss, he needs to be

> **FEEDING TIPS**
> You will probably start feeding your pup the same food that he has been getting from the breeder; the breeder should give you a few days' supply to start you off. Although you should not give your pup too many treats, you will want to have puppy treats on hand for coaxing, training, rewards, etc. Be careful, though, as a small pup's calorie requirements are relatively low and a few treats can add up to almost a full day's worth of calories without the required nutrition.

comfortable in his crate. On that note, it is extremely important that the crate is never used as a form of punishment, or the pup will develop a negative association with the crate.

Accustom the pup to the crate in short, gradually increasing time intervals in which you put him in the crate, maybe with a treat, and stay in the room with him. If he cries or makes a fuss, do not go to him, but stay in his sight. Gradually he will realize that staying in his crate is okay without your help, and it will not be so traumatic for him when you are not around. You may want to leave the radio on softly when you leave the house; the sound of human voices may be comforting to him.

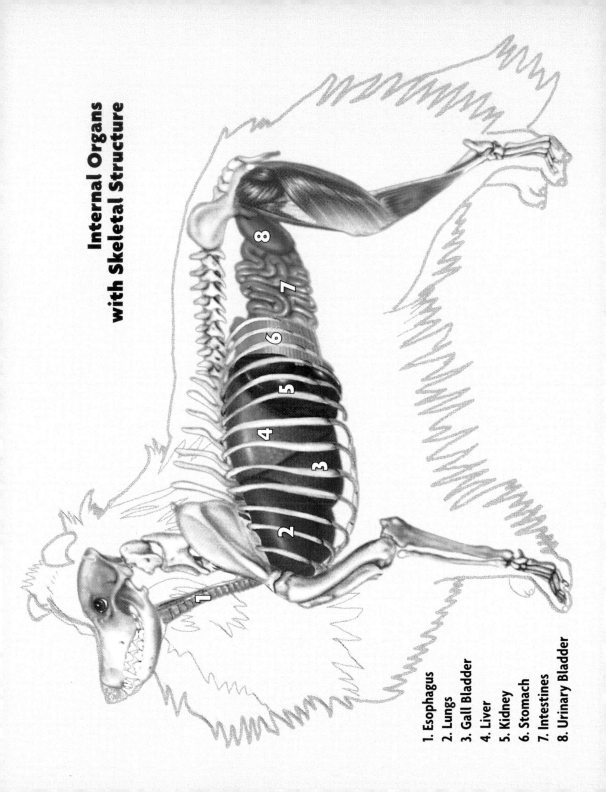

Internal Organs
with Skeletal Structure

1. Esophagus
2. Lungs
3. Gall Bladder
4. Liver
5. Kidney
6. Stomach
7. Intestines
8. Urinary Bladder

DIETARY AND FEEDING CONSIDERATIONS

Today the choices of food for your Shetland Sheepdog are many and varied. There are simply dozens of brands of food in all sorts of flavors and textures, ranging from puppy diets to those for seniors. There are even hypoallergenic and low-calorie diets available. Because your Sheltie's food has a bearing on coat, health and temperament, it is essential that the most suitable diet is selected for a Sheltie of his age. It is fair to say, however, that even dedicated owners can be somewhat perplexed by the enormous range of foods available. Only understanding what is best for your dog will help you reach an informed decision.

Dog foods are produced in three basic types: dry, semi-moist and canned. Dry foods are useful for the cost-conscious, for overall they tend to be less expensive than semi-moist or canned. Dry foods contain the least fat and the most preservatives. In general, canned foods are made up of 60–70% water, while semi-moist ones often contain so much sugar that they are perhaps the least preferred by owners, even though their dogs seem to like them.

When selecting your dog's diet, three stages of development must be considered: the puppy

FOOD PREFERENCE

Selecting the best dry dog food is difficult. There is no majority consensus among veterinary scientists as to the value of nutrient analysis (protein, fat, fiber, moisture, ash, cholesterol, minerals, etc.). All agree that feeding trials are what matter most, but you also have to consider the individual dog. The dog's weight, age and activity level, and what pleases his taste, all must be considered. It is probably best to take the advice of your veterinarian. Every dog's dietary requirements vary, even during the lifetime of a particular dog.

If your dog is fed a good dry food, he does not require supplements of meat or vegetables. Dogs do appreciate a little variety in their diets, so you may choose to stay with the same brand but vary the flavor. Alternatively, you may wish to add a little flavored stock to give a difference to the taste.

stage, the adult stage and the senior stage.

PUPPY DIET

Puppies instinctively want to suck milk from their mother's teats and a normal puppy will exhibit this behavior from just a few moments following birth. If puppies do not attempt to suckle within the first half-hour or so, they should be encouraged to do so by placing them on the nipples, having selected ones with plenty of milk. This early milk supply is impor-tant in providing colostrum to protect the puppies during the first eight to ten weeks of their lives. Although a mother's milk is much better than any milk formula, despite there being some excellent ones available, if the puppies do not feed, the breeder will have to feed them himself. For those with less experience, advice from a veterinarian is important so that not only the right quantity of milk but also that of correct quality is fed, at suit-ably frequent intervals, usually every two hours during the first few days of life.

Puppies should be allowed to nurse from their mothers for about the first six weeks, although from the third or fourth week the breeder will begin to introduce small portions of suitable solid food. Most breeders like to intro-duce alternate milk and meat meals initially, building up to weaning time.

By the time the puppies are seven or a maximum of eight weeks old, they should be fully weaned and fed solely on a proprietary puppy food. Selection of the most suitable, good-quality diet at this time is essential, for a puppy's fastest growth rate is during the first year of life. Veterinarians and are able to offer advice in this regard. The frequency of meals will be reduced over time and the puppy can stay on the puppy diet until around one year of age, depending

---

FEEDING TIPS

- Dog food must be served at room temperature, neither too hot nor too cold. Fresh water, changed often and served in a clean bowl, is mandatory, especially when feeding dry food.
- Never feed your dog from the table while you are eating, and never feed your dog leftovers from your own meal. They usually contain too much fat and too much seasoning.
- Dogs must chew their food. Hard pellets are excellent; soups and stews are to be avoided.
- Don't add leftovers or any extras to commercial dog food. The normal food is usually balanced, and adding something extra destroys the balance.
- Except for age-related changes, dogs do not require dietary variations. They can be fed the same diet, day after day, without becoming bored or ill.

A Worthy Investment

Veterinary studies have proven that a balanced high-quality diet
pays off in your dog's coat quality, behavior and activity level.
Invest in premium brands for the maximum payoff with your dog.

on the diet fed and the individual dog's development.

Puppy and junior diets should be well balanced for the needs of your dog, so that, except in certain circumstances, additional vitamins, minerals and proteins will not be required.

ADULT DIET

A dog is considered an adult when he has stopped growing, and this varies from dog to dog. Again you should rely upon your veterinarian or breeder to recommend an acceptable maintenance diet and to advise you about when to switch your Sheltie from a puppy to adult food. Major dog-food manufacturers specialize in this type of food, and it is just necessary for you to select the one best suited to your dog's needs. Active dogs may have different requirements than sedate dogs.

SENIOR DIET

As dogs get older, their metabolism changes. The older dog usually exercises less, moves more slowly and sleeps more. This change in lifestyle and physiological performance requires a change in diet. Since these changes take place slowly, they might not be recognizable. What is easily recognizable is weight gain. By continuing to feed your dog an adult-maintenance diet when he is slowing down metabolically, your dog will gain weight. Obesity in an older dog compounds the health problems that already accompany old age.

As your dog gets older, few of his organs function up to par. The kidneys slow down and the intestines become less efficient. These age-related factors are best handled with a change in diet and a change in feeding schedule to give smaller portions that are more easily digested.

There is no single best diet for every older dog. While many dogs do well on light or senior diets, other dogs do better on puppy diets or other special premium

STORING DOG FOOD

You must store your dry dog food carefully. Open packages of dog food quickly lose their vitamin value, usually within 90 days of being opened. Mold spores and vermin could also contaminate the food.

diets such as lamb and rice. Be sensitive to your senior Sheltie's diet and this will help control other problems that may arise with your old friend.

WATER

Just as your dog needs proper nutrition from his food, water is an essential "nutrient" as well. Water keeps the dog's body properly hydrated and promotes normal function of the body's systems. During housebreaking, it is necessary to keep an eye on how much water your Sheltie is drinking, but once he is reliably trained, he should have access to clean fresh water at all times. Make sure that the dog's water bowl is clean, and change the water often, making sure that water is always available for your dog, especially if you feed dry food.

EXERCISE

Although a Shetland Sheepdog is small, he is an energetic dog that requires ample exercise. A sedentary lifestyle is as harmful to a dog as it is to a person. The Sheltie is an active breed that enjoys exercise, but you don't have to be an Olympic athlete to provide your dog with the activity he needs. Regular walks, play sessions in the yard or letting the dog run free in an enclosed area under your supervision are sufficient forms of exercise for the Sheltie. For those who are more

ambitious, you will find that your Sheltie also enjoys long walks, an occasional hike or even a swim! Bear in mind that an overweight dog should never be suddenly over-exercised; instead, he should be allowed to increase exercise

A balanced diet is absolutely essential, especially during your Sheltie's crucial growth period, to ensure proper development of bone and muscle.

GRAIN-BASED DIETS

Some less expensive dog foods are based on grains and other plant proteins. While these products may appear to be attractively priced, many breeders prefer a diet based on animal proteins and believe that they are more conducive to your dog's health. Many grain-based diets rely on soy protein, which may cause flatulence (passing gas).

There are many cases, however, when your dog might require a special diet. These special requirements should only be recommended by your veterinarian.

Shelties. A pet-supply store will
have in stock the appropriate
items for use on Shelties, so be
sure to tell the shopkeeper for
which breed of dog you are shop-
ping for supplies.

Everyday care of the Sheltie

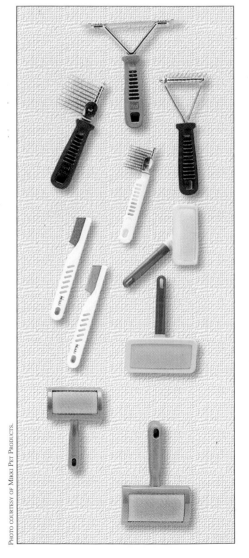

slowly. Also remember that exercise is not only essential to keep
the dog's body fit, it is essential to
his mental well being. A bored
dog will find something to do,
which often manifests itself in
some type of destructive behavior.
In this sense, it is essential for the
owner's mental well-being as
well!

GROOMING

BRUSHING
A metal comb and a natural bristle brush designed for use on long
coats are necessities for grooming

There are no limitations to the kinds of exercise your Sheltie will welcome. If you are fortunate enough to have a treadmill, you can train your Sheltie to use it safely. This is especially useful in inclement weather.

means that you will be brushing him daily. Daily brushing is effective for removing dead hair and stimulating the dog's natural oils to add shine and a healthy look to the coat. If you brush your Sheltie regularly, he will not get matted; therefore, the brushing will take only minutes because there are no mats with which to contend. If taught to stand still or lie down for a short daily brushing session, your Sheltie will come to love grooming time and look forward to a biscuit when the process is completed. Regular grooming sessions are also a good way to spend time with your dog.

BATHING

Dogs do not need to be bathed as often as humans, but bathing as needed is essential for healthy skin and a healthy, shiny coat. Again, like most anything, if you accustom your pup to being bathed as a puppy, it will be second nature by the time he

This is the proper way to lift a Sheltie into the tub. He is being taken to his bath and he looks a bit hesitant!

Wet the dog thoroughly before applying the dog shampoo. Be sure to keep the dog's head and ears from the spray of the nozzle.

grows up. You want your dog to be at ease in the bathtub or else it could end up a wet, soapy, messy ordeal for both of you!

Brush your Sheltie thoroughly before wetting his coat. This will get rid of most mats and tangles, which are harder to remove when the coat is wet. Make that your dog has a good non-slip surface to stand on. Begin by wetting the dog's coat. A shower or hose attachment is necessary for thoroughly wetting and rinsing the coat. Check the water temperature to make sure that it is neither too hot nor too cold for the dog.

Next, apply shampoo to the

dog's coat and work it into a good lather. You should purchase a shampoo that is made for dogs. Do not use a product made for human hair. Wash the head last; you do not want shampoo to drip into the dog's eyes while you are washing the rest of his body. Work the shampoo all the way down to the skin. You can use this opportunity to check the skin for any bumps, bites or other abnormalities. Do not neglect any area of the body—get all of the hard-to-reach places.

Once the dog has been thoroughly shampooed, he requires an equally thorough rinsing. Shampoo left in the coat can be irritat-

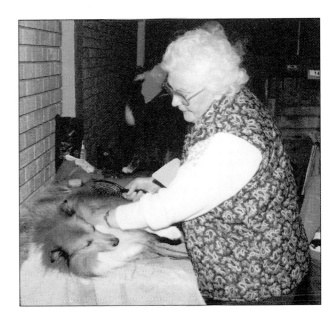

SOAP IT UP
The use of human soap products like shampoo, bubble bath and hand soap can be damaging to a dog's coat and skin. Human products are too strong; they remove the protective oils coating the dog's hair and skin that make him water-resistant. Use only shampoo made especially for dogs. You may like to use a medicated shampoo, which will help to keep external parasites at bay.

ing to the skin. Protect his eyes from the shampoo by shielding them with your hand and directing the flow of water in the opposite direction. You should also avoid getting water in the ear canal. Be prepared for your dog to shake out his coat—you might want to stand back, but make sure you have a hold on the dog to keep him from running through the house, and have a towel ready.

Ear Cleaning
The ears should be kept clean and any excess hair inside the ear should be carefully removed. Ears must always be kept clean. This can be done using a special canine ear cleaner with cotton balls or cotton swabs. Many people use cotton swabs, but

Your Sheltie should be brushed every day in order to keep his coat from matting and knotting, and to remove any loose hairs. You will need to teach the Sheltie to lie down on his side for part of the grooming ritual.

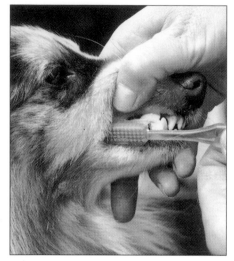

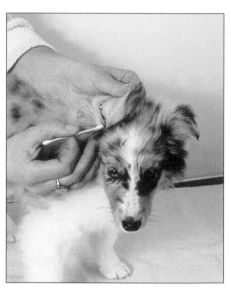

Cleaning your dog's teeth is also a part of the grooming process. Ask your vet about proper maintenance of your dog's teeth. While brushing can be done at home, scaling is usually done at the vet's office.

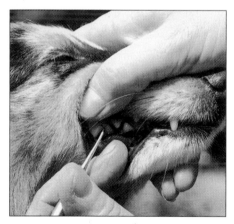

Be very careful if using a cotton swab; never poke or prod, and never enter the ear canal.

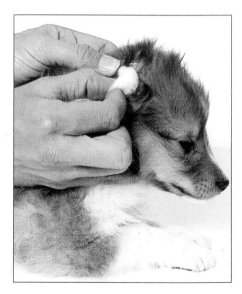

Gently wipe around the Sheltie's eyes with a cotton ball.

A cotton ball is the best option for cleaning the Sheltie's ears. The ear should also be examined for any abnormalities as you clean.

extreme care must be taken not to delve into the ear canals as this can cause injury. Be on the lookout for any signs of infection or ear-mite infestation. If your Sheltie has been shaking his head or scratching at his ears frequently, this usually indicates a problem. If his ears have an unusual odor, this is a sure sign of mite infestation or infection, and a signal to have his ears checked by the vet.

NAIL CLIPPING

Your Sheltie should be accustomed to having his nails trimmed at an early age, since it will be part of your maintenance routine throughout his life. Not only does it look nicer, but long nails can scratch someone unintentionally. Also, a long nail has a better chance of ripping and bleeding, or causing the feet to spread. A good rule of thumb is that if you can hear your dog's nails' clicking on the floor when he walks, his nails are too long.

Before you start cutting, make sure you can identify the "quick" in each nail. The quick is a blood vessel that runs through the center of each nail and grows rather close to the end. It will bleed if accidentally cut, which will be quite painful for the dog as it contains nerve endings. Keep some type of clotting agent on hand, such as a styptic pencil or styptic powder (the type used for

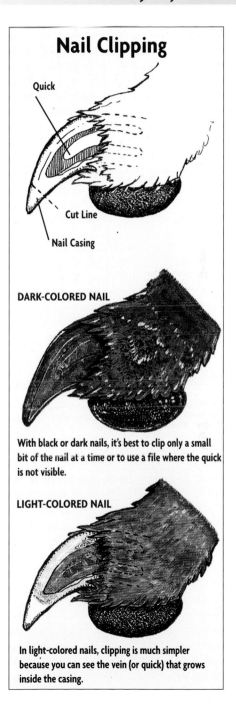

Nail Clipping

Quick

Cut Line

Nail Casing

DARK-COLORED NAIL

With black or dark nails, it's best to clip only a small bit of the nail at a time or to use a file where the quick is not visible.

LIGHT-COLORED NAIL

In light-colored nails, clipping is much simpler because you can see the vein (or quick) that grows inside the casing.

Your dog's nails should be trimmed regularly. Dogs that run on hard surfaces usually wear their nails down and don't require clipping as often as dogs who exercise mostly on grass.

shaving). This will stop the bleeding quickly when applied to the end of the cut nail. Do not panic if this happens, just stop the bleeding and talk soothingly to your dog. Once he has calmed down, move on to the next nail. It is better to clip a little at a time, particularly with black-nailed dogs.

Opposite page: Typical hairs enlarged hundreds of times their natural size. The cuticle (outer covering) is very clean. The inset shows the growing tip.

GROOMING EQUIPMENT

Visit your local pet shop to purchase top-quality grooming equipment for your Sheltie.
- Natural bristle brush
- Slicker brush
- Metal comb
- Scissors
- Rubber mat
- Dog shampoo
- Spray hose attachment
- Blow dryer
- Towels
- Ear cleaner
- Cotton balls and swabs
- Nail clippers
- Styptic pencil

Hold your pup steady as you begin trimming his nails; you do not want him to make any sudden movements or run away. Talk to him soothingly and stroke him as you clip. Holding his foot in your hand, simply take off the end of each nail in one quick clip. You can purchase nail clippers that are specially made for dogs; you can probably find them wherever you buy grooming or other pet supplies.

TRAVELING WITH YOUR DOG

CAR TRAVEL

You should accustom your Sheltie to riding in a car at an early age. You may or may not take him in the car often, but at the very least he will need to go to the vet and you do not want these trips to be traumatic for the dog or a big hassle for you. The safest way for a dog to ride in the car is in his crate. If he uses a crate in the house, you can use the same crate for travel.

Put the pup in the crate and see how he reacts. If he seems uneasy, you can have a passenger hold him on his lap while you drive. Another option is a specially made safety harness for dogs, which straps the dog in much like a seat belt. Do not let the dog roam loose in the vehicle—this is very dangerous! If you should stop short, your dog can be thrown and injured. If the dog

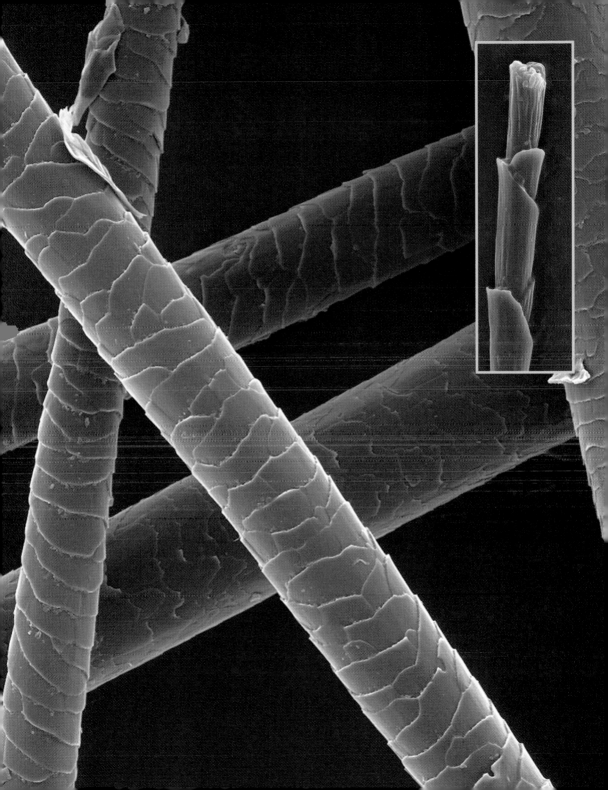

Wire or fiberglass crates are ideal for car travel. It is always recommended to use a crate for travel. It is the safest way to transport a Sheltie or any dog.

starts climbing on you and pestering you while you are driving, you will not be able to concentrate on the road. It is an unsafe situation for everyone—human and canine.

For long trips, be prepared to stop to let the dog relieve himself. Bring along whatever you need to clean up after him. You should take along some paper towels and some rags for use should he have an accident in the car or suffer from travel sickness.

AIR TRAVEL

Contact your chosen airline before proceeding with your travel plans that include your Sheltie. The dog will be required to travel in a fiberglass crate and you should always check in advance with the airline regarding specific requirements for the crate's size, type and

TRAVELING ABROAD

For international travel you will have to make arrangements well in advance (perhaps months), as countries' regulations pertaining to bringing in animals differ. There may be special health certificates and/or vaccinations that your dog will need before taking the trip; sometimes this has to be done within a certain time frame. In rabies-free countries, you will need to bring proof of the dog's rabies vaccination and there may be a quarantine period upon arrival.

labeling, as well as any travel restrictions. To help put the dog at ease, give him one of his favorite toys in the crate. Do not feed the dog for several hours prior to checking in so that you minimize his need to relieve himself. Some airlines require you to provide documentation as to when the dog has last been fed. In any case, a light meal is best. For long trips, you will have to attach food and water bowls to the dog's crate so that airline employees can tend to him between legs of the trip.

VACATIONS AND BOARDING

So you want to take a family vacation—and you want to include *all* members of the family. You would probably make arrangements for accommodations ahead of time anyway, but this is especially important when traveling with a dog. You do not want to make an overnight stop at the only place around for miles and find out that they do not allow dogs. Also, you do not want to reserve a place for your family without confirming that you are traveling with a dog because, if it is against their policy, you may not have a place to stay.

Alternatively, if you are traveling and choose not to bring your Sheltie, you will have to make arrangements for him while you are away. Some options are to take him to a friend's house to stay while you are gone, to have a trusted friend stop by often or stay at your house or to bring your dog to a reputable boarding kennel. If you choose to board him at a kennel, you should visit

in advance to see the facilities, how clean they are and where the dogs are kept. Talk to some of the employees and see how they treat the dogs—do they spend time with the dogs, play with

Should you find it necessary to board your Sheltie, look for a kennel that is close by, clean, and spacious with ample exercise opportunities for your dog. Your vet can usually give you good advice about a suitable kennel for boarding.

No matter what your Sheltie tells you, traveling by crate is the only way to go!

ON THE ROAD

If you are going on a long car trip with your dog, be sure the hotels are dog-friendly. Many hotels do not accept dogs. Also take along some ice that can be thawed and offered to your dog if he becomes overheated. Most dogs like to lick ice.

them, exercise and groom them, etc.? Also find out the kennel's policy on vaccinations and what they require. This is for all of the dogs' safety, since when dogs are kept together, there is a greater risk of diseases being passed from dog to dog.

IDENTIFICATION

Your Sheltie is your valued companion and friend. That is why you always keep a close eye on him and you have made sure that he cannot escape from the yard or wriggle out of his collar and run away from you. However, accidents can happen and there may come a time when your dog unexpectedly gets separated from you. If this unfortu-

COLLAR REQUIRED

If your dog gets lost, he is not able to ask for directions home. Identification tags fastened to the collar give important information—the dog's name, the owner's name, the owner's address and a telephone number where the owner can be reached. This makes it easy for whomever finds the dog to contact the owner and arrange to have the dog returned. An added advantage is that a person will be more likely to approach a lost dog who has ID tags on his collar; it tells the person that this is somebody's pet rather than a stray. This is the easiest and fastest method of identification, provided that the tags stay on the collar and the collar stays on the dog.

A breeder has a huge responsibility to his Sheltie "flock" to keep them safe and secure, and to care for each dog and pup properly, according to age and stage of development.

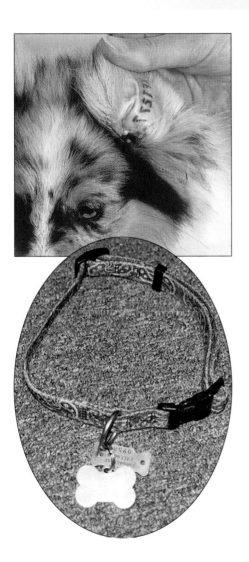

IDENTIFICATION OPTIONS

As puppies become more and more expensive, especially those puppies of high quality for showing and/or breeding, they have a greater chance of being stolen. The usual collar dog tag is, of course, easily removed. But there are two more permanent techniques that have become widely used for identification.

The puppy microchip implantation involves the injection of a small microchip, about the size of a corn kernel, under the skin of the dog. If your dog shows up at a clinic or shelter, or is offered for resale under less-than-savory circumstances, he can be positively identified by the microchip. The microchip is scanned, and a registry quickly identifies you as the owner.

Tattooing is done on various parts of the dog, from his belly to his ears. The number tattooed can be your telephone number, the dog's registration number or any other number that you can easily memorize. When professional dog thieves see a tattooed dog, they usually lose interest. For the safety of our dogs, no laboratory facility or dog broker will accept a tattooed dog as stock.

Discuss microchipping and tattooing with your vet and breeder. Some vets perform these services on their own premises for a reasonable fee. To ensure that your dog's ID is effective, be certain that the dog is then properly registered with a legitimate national database.

Tattoos have become a very common method of permanently identifying a dog. With a long-haired breed, the ear is the location that is frequently chosen. ID tags and licenses should be attached to the dog's everyday collar.

nate event should occur, the first thing on your mind will be finding him. Proper identification, including an ID tag and possibly a tattoo and/or a microchip, will increase the chances of his being returned to you safely and quickly.

TRAINING YOUR
SHETLAND SHEEPDOG

Training a single Sheltie is certainly more manageable than a half dozen! These six well-trained dogs walk nicely by their mistress's side.

Living with an untrained dog is a lot like owning a piano that you do not know how to play—it is a nice object to look at, but it does not do much more than that to bring you pleasure. Now try taking piano lessons, and suddenly the piano comes alive and brings forth magical sounds and rhythms that set your heart singing and your body swaying.

The same is true with your Shetland Sheepdog. Any dog is a big responsibility and, if not trained sensibly, may develop unacceptable behavior that annoys you or could even cause family friction.

To train your Shetland Sheepdog, you may like to enroll in an obedience

HONOR AND OBEY
Dogs are the most honorable animals in existence. They consider another species (humans) as their own. They interface with you. You are their leader. Puppies perceive children to be on their level; their actions around small children are different from their behavior around their adult masters.

class. Teach him good manners as you learn how and why he behaves the way he does. Find out how to communicate with your dog and how to recognize and understand his communications with you. Suddenly the dog takes on a new role in your life—he is smart, interesting, well behaved and fun to be with. He demonstrates his bond of devotion to you daily. In other words, your Shetland Sheepdog does wonders for your ego

A politely posing bunch in the rainbow of Sheltie colors. Training dogs in puppyhood helps develop adults that behave picture-perfect.

because he constantly reminds you that you are not only his leader, you are his hero!

Those involved with teaching dog obedience and counseling owners about their dogs' behavior have discovered some interesting facts about dog ownership. For example, training dogs when they are puppies results in the highest rate of success in developing well-mannered and well-adjusted adult dogs. Training an older dog, from six months to six years of age, can produce almost equal results, providing that the owner accepts the dog's slower rate of learning capability and is willing to work patiently to help the dog succeed at developing to his fullest potential. Unfortunately, many owners of untrained adult dogs lack the patience factor, so they do not persist until their dogs are successful at learning particular behaviors.

THINK BEFORE YOU BARK

Dogs are sensitive to their masters' moods and emotions. Use your voice wisely when communicating with your dog. Never raise your voice at your dog unless you are trying to correct him. "Barking" at your dog can become as meaningless as "dogspeak" is to you.

Young puppies are better students than adolescent puppies. As soon as a dog's hormones start flowing, he is easily distracted and has other interests in life.

Training a puppy aged 10 to 16 weeks (20 weeks at the most) is like working with a dry sponge in a pool of water. The pup soaks up whatever you show him and constantly looks for more things to do and learn. At this early age, his body is not yet producing hormones, and therein lies the reason for such a high rate of success. Without hormones, he is focused on his owners and not particularly interested in investigating other places, dogs, people, etc. You are his leader: his provider of food, water, shelter and security. He latches onto you and wants to stay close. He will usually follow you from room to room, will not let you out of his sight when you are outdoors with him and will respond in like manner to the people and animals you encounter. If you greet a friend warmly, he will be happy to greet the person as well. If, however, you are hesitant or anxious about the approach of a stranger, he will respond accordingly.

Once the puppy begins to produce hormones, his natural curiosity emerges and he begins to investigate the world around him. It is at this time when you may notice that the untrained dog begins to wander away from you and even ignore your commands to stay close. When this behavior becomes a problem, the owner has two choices: get rid of the dog or train him. It is strongly urged that you choose the latter option.

There are usually classes within a reasonable distance from your home, but you also can do a lot to train your dog yourself. Sometimes there are classes available but the tuition is too costly. Whatever the circumstances, the solution to training your Sheltie without formal obedience classes lies within the pages of this book.

This chapter is devoted to helping you train your Shetland Sheepdog at home. If the recommended procedures are followed faithfully, you may expect positive results that will prove rewarding to both you and your dog.

Whether your new charge is a puppy or a mature adult, the

methods of teaching and the
techniques we use in training
basic behaviors are the same.
After all, no dog, whether puppy
or adult, likes harsh or inhu-
mane methods. All creatures,
however, respond favorably to
gentle motivational methods and
sincere praise and encouragement. Now let us get started.

HOUSEBREAKING

You can train a puppy to relieve
himself wherever you choose,
but this must be somewhere
suitable. You should bear in
mind from the outset that when
your puppy is old enough to go
out in public places, any canine
droppings must be removed at
once. You will always have to
carry with you a small plastic
bag or "poop-scoop."

Outdoor training includes
such surfaces as grass, dirt and
cement. Indoor training usually
means training your dog to
newspaper. When deciding on
the surface and location that you
will want your Shetland Sheepdog to use, be sure it is going to
be permanent. Training your dog
to grass and then changing your
mind two months later is
extremely difficult for both dog
and owner.

Next, choose the command
you will use each and every
time you want your puppy to
void. "Go hurry up" and "Go
make" are examples of

PARENTAL GUIDANCE
Training a dog is a life experience.
Many parents admit that much of
what they know about raising children
they learned from caring for their
dogs. Dogs respond to love, fairness
and guidance, just as children do.
Become a good dog owner and you
may become an even better parent.

Your Sheltie pup begins socialization with his littermates and continues with his new owners. This is an essential part of early training.

Take your puppy out often—every hour for an eight-week-old, for example, and always immediately after sleeping and eating. The older the puppy, the less often he will need to relieve himself. Finally, as a mature healthy adult, he will require only three to five relief trips per day.

HOUSING

Since the types of housing and control you provide for your puppy have a direct relationship on the success of house-training, we consider the various aspects of both before we begin training.

Bringing a new puppy home and turning him loose in your house can be compared to turning a child loose in a sports arena and telling the child that the place is all his! The sheer enormity of the place would be too much for him to handle.

Instead, offer the puppy clearly defined areas where he can play, sleep, eat and live. A room of the house where the family gathers is the most obvious choice. Puppies are social

commands commonly used by dog owners.

Get in the habit of giving the puppy your chosen relief command before you take him out. That way, when he becomes an adult, you will be able to determine if he wants to go out when you ask him. A confirmation will be signs of interest, such as wagging his tail, watching you intently, circling around, going to the door, etc.

PUPPY'S NEEDS

The puppy needs to relieve himself after play periods, after each meal, after he has been sleeping and any time he indicates that he is looking for a place to urinate or defecate. The urinary and intestinal tract muscles of very young puppies are not fully developed. Therefore, like human babies, puppies need to relieve themselves frequently.

ATTENTION!

Your dog is actually training you at the same time you are training him. Dogs do things to get attention. They usually repeat whatever succeeds in getting your attention.

animals and need to feel a part of the pack right from the start. Hearing your voice, watching you while you are doing things and smelling you nearby are all positive reinforcers that he is now a member of your pack. Usually a family room, the kitchen or a nearby adjoining breakfast area is ideal for providing safety and security for both puppy and owner.

Within that room, there should be a smaller area that the puppy can call his own. An alcove, a wire or fiberglass dog crate or a gated (not boarded!) corner from which he can view the activities of his new family will be fine. The size of the area or crate is the key factor here.

Training must be reinforced throughout the Sheltie's life. Practicing commands should be a part of your dog's everyday life.

PAPER CAPER

Never line your pup's sleeping area with newspaper. Puppy litters are usually raised on newspaper and, once in your home, the puppy will immediately associate newspaper with voiding. Never put newspaper on any floor while house-training, as this will only confuse the puppy. If you are paper-training him, use paper in his designated relief area only. Finally, restrict water intake after evening meals. Offer a few licks at a time—never let a young puppy gulp water after meals.

The area must be large enough for the puppy to lie down and stretch out as well as stand up without rubbing his head on the top, yet small enough so that he cannot relieve himself at one end and sleep at the other without coming into contact with his droppings before he is fully trained to relieve himself outside. Dogs are, by nature, clean animals and will not remain close to their relief areas unless forced to do so. In those cases, they then become dirty dogs and usually remain that way for life.

The designated area should be lined with clean bedding and

HOUSE-TRAINING TIP

Most of all, be consistent. Always take your dog to the same location, always use the same command and always have the dog on leash when he is in his relief area, unless a fenced-in yard is available.

By following the Success Method, your puppy will be completely house-broken by the time his muscle and brain development reach maturity. Keep in mind that small breeds usually mature faster than large breeds, but all puppies should be trained by six months of age.

a toy. Water must always be available, in a non-spill container, but be aware of your pup's water intake so you will know when he needs "to go."

CONTROL

By *control*, we mean helping the puppy to create a lifestyle pattern that will be compatible to that of his human pack *(you!)*. Just as we guide little children to learn our way of life, we must show the puppy when it is time to play, eat, sleep, exercise and even entertain himself.

Your puppy should always sleep in his crate. He should also learn that, during times of household confusion and excessive human activity such as at breakfast when family members are preparing for the day, he can play by himself in relative safety and comfort in his designated area. Each time you leave the puppy alone, he should understand exactly where he is to stay. Puppies are chewers. They cannot tell the difference between things like lamp cords, television wires, shoes, table legs, etc. Chewing into a television wire, for example, can be fatal to the puppy, while a shorted wire can start a fire in the house.

If the puppy chews on the arm of the chair when he is alone, you will probably discipline him angrily when you get home. Thus, he makes the association that your coming home means he is going to be punished. (He will not remember chewing the chair and is incapable of making the association of the discipline with his naughty deed.) Keeping the puppy crated when you can't be there to supervise prevents him from engaging in destructive and possibly dangerous behavior.

Times of excitement, such as family parties, etc., can be fun for the puppy providing he can view the activities from the security of his designated area. He is not underfoot and he is not being fed all sorts of tidbits that will probably cause him stomach distress, yet he still feels a part of the fun.

SCHEDULE

A puppy should be taken to his relief area each time he is released from his designated area, after meals, after play sessions, when he first awakens in the morning (at age eight weeks, this can mean 5 a.m.!). The puppy will indicate that he's ready "to go" by circling or sniffing busily—do not misinterpret these signs. For a puppy less than ten weeks of age, a routine of taking him out every hour is necessary. As the puppy grows, he will be able to wait for longer periods of time.

Keep trips to his relief area

THE CLEAN LIFE

By providing sleeping and resting quarters that fit the dog, and offering frequent opportunities to relieve himself outside his quarters, the puppy quickly learns that the outdoors (or the newspaper if you are training him to paper) is the place to go when he needs to urinate or defecate. It also reinforces his innate desire to keep his sleeping quarters clean. This, in turn, helps develop the muscle control that will eventually produce a dog with clean living habits.

short. Stay no more than five or six minutes and then return to the house. If he goes during that time, praise him lavishly and take him indoors immediately. If he does not, but he has an accident when you go back indoors, pick him up immediately, say "No! No!" and return to his relief area. Wait a few minutes, then return to the house again. Never hit a puppy or put his face in urine or excrement when he has an accident!

Once indoors, put the puppy in his crate until you have had time to clean up his accident. Then release him to the family area and watch him more closely than before. Chances are, his accident was a result of your not picking up his signal or waiting too long before offering him the opportunity to relieve himself. Never hold a grudge against the puppy for accidents.

Let the puppy learn that going outdoors means it is time to relieve himself, not play. Once trained, he will be able to play indoors and out and still differentiate between the times for

THE SUCCESS METHOD

Success that comes by luck is usually short-lived. Success that comes by well-thought-out proven methods is often more easily achieved and permanent. This is the Success Method. It is designed to give you, the puppy owner, a simple yet proven way to help your puppy develop clean living habits and a feeling of security in his new environment.

6 Steps to Successful Crate Training

1 Tell the puppy "Crate time!" and place him in the crate with a small treat (a piece of cheese or half of a biscuit). Let him stay in the crate for five minutes while you are in the same room. Then release him and praise lavishly. Never release him when he is fussing. Wait until he is quiet before you let him out.

2 Repeat Step 1 several times a day.

3 The next day, place the puppy in the crate as before. Let him stay there for ten minutes. Do this several times.

4 Continue building time in five-minute increments until the puppy stays in his crate for 30 minutes with you in the room. Always take him to his relief area after prolonged periods in his crate.

5 Now go back to Step 1 and let the puppy stay in his crate for five minutes, this time while you are out of the room.

6 Once again, build crate time in five-minute increments with you out of the room. When the puppy will stay willingly in his crate (he may even fall asleep!) for 30 minutes with you out of the room, he will be ready to stay in it for several hours at a time.

play versus the times for relief.

Help him develop regular hours for naps, being alone, playing by himself and just resting, all in his crate. Encourage him to entertain himself while you are busy with your activities. Let him learn that having you near is comforting, but it is not your main purpose in life to provide him with undivided attention.

Each time you put your puppy in his own area, use the same command, whatever suits best. Soon, he will run to his crate or special area when he hears you say those words.

Crate training provides safety for you, the puppy and the home. It also provides the puppy with a feeling of security, and that helps the puppy achieve self-confidence and clean habits. Remember that one of the primary ingredients in house-training your puppy is control. Regardless of your lifestyle, there will always be occasions when you will need to have a place where your dog can stay and be happy and safe. Crate training is the answer for now and in the future.

In conclusion, a few key elements are really all you need for a successful house-training method—consistency, frequency, praise, control and supervision. By following these procedures with a normal, healthy puppy, you and the puppy will soon be past the stage of accidents and ready to move on to a full and rewarding life together.

Without structure and discipline, the world of canines would be chaotic and not very photogenic!

ROLES OF DISCIPLINE, REWARD AND PUNISHMENT

Discipline, training one to act in accordance with rules, brings order to life. It is as simple as that. Without discipline, particularly in a group society, chaos reigns supreme and the group will eventually perish. Humans and canines are social animals and need some form of discipline in order to function effectively. They must procure food, reproduce to keep their species going and protect their home base and their young.

If there were no discipline in the lives of social animals, they would eventually die from starvation and/or predation by other stronger animals. In the case of domestic canines, dogs need discipline in their lives in order to understand how their pack (you and other family members) functions and how they must act in order to survive.

A large humane society in a highly populated area recently surveyed dog owners regarding their satisfaction with their relationships with their dogs. People who had trained their dogs were 75% more satisfied with their pets than those who had never trained their dogs.

Dr. Edward Thorndike, a noted psychologist, established *Thorndike's Theory of Learning*, which states that a behavior that results in a pleasant event tends to be repeated. Likewise, a behavior that results in an unpleasant event tends not to be repeated. It is this theory on which training methods are based today. For example, if you manipulate a dog to perform a specific behavior and reward him for doing it, he is likely to do it again because he enjoyed the end result.

Occasionally, punishment, a penalty inflicted for an offense, is necessary. The best type of punishment often comes from an outside source. For example, a child is told not to touch the stove because he may get burned. He disobeys and touches the stove. In doing so, he receives a burn. From that time on, he respects the heat of the stove and avoids contact with it. Therefore, a behavior that results in an unpleasant event tends not to be repeated.

LET'S GET PHYSICAL!

The puppy should also have regular play and exercise sessions when he is with you or a family member. Exercise for a very young puppy can consist of a short walk around the house or yard. Playing can include fetching games with a large ball or a special toy. (All puppies teethe and need soft things upon which to chew.) Remember to restrict play periods to indoors within his living area (the family room, for example) until he is completely house-trained.

CANINE DEVELOPMENT SCHEDULE

It is important to understand how and at what age a puppy develops into adulthood.
If you are a puppy owner, consult the following Canine Development Schedule to
determine the stage of development your puppy is currently experiencing.
This knowledge will help you as you work with the puppy in the weeks and months ahead.

Period	Age	Characteristics
FIRST TO THIRD	**BIRTH TO SEVEN WEEKS**	Puppy needs food, sleep and warmth, and responds to simple and gentle touching. Needs mother for security and disciplining. Needs littermates for learning and interacting with other dogs. Pup learns to function within a pack and learns pack order of dominance. Begin socializing pup with adults and children for short periods. Pup begins to become aware of his environment.
FOURTH	**EIGHT TO TWELVE WEEKS**	Brain is fully developed. Needs socializing with outside world. Remove from mother and littermates. Needs to change from canine pack to human pack. Human dominance necessary. Fear period occurs between 8 and 12 weeks. Avoid fright and pain.
FIFTH	**THIRTEEN TO SIXTEEN WEEKS**	Training and formal obedience should begin. Less association with other dogs, more with people, places, situations. Period will pass easily if you remember this is pup's change-to-adolescence time. Be firm and fair. Flight instinct prominent. Permissiveness and over-disciplining can do permanent damage. Praise for good behavior.
JUVENILE	**FOUR TO EIGHT MONTHS**	Another fear period about 7 to 8 months of age. It passes quickly, but be cautious of fright and pain. Sexual maturity reached. Dominant traits established. Dog should understand sit, down, come and stay by now.

NOTE: THESE ARE APPROXIMATE TIME FRAMES. ALLOW FOR INDIVIDUAL DIFFERENCES IN PUPPIES.

A good example of a dog learning the hard way is the dog who chases the house cat. He is told many times to leave the cat alone, yet he persists in teasing the cat. Then, one day he begins chasing the cat but the cat turns and swipes a claw across the dog's face, leaving him with a painful gash on his nose. The final result is that the dog stops chasing the cat.

TRAINING EQUIPMENT

COLLAR AND LEASH
For a Shetland Sheepdog, the collar and leash that you use for training must be one with which you are easily able to work, not too heavy for the dog and perfectly safe.

TREATS
Have a bag of treats on hand. Something nutritious and easy to swallow works best. Use a soft treat, a chunk of cheese or a piece of cooked chicken rather than a dry biscuit. By the time the dog gets done chewing a dry treat, he will forget why he is being rewarded in the first place! Using food rewards will not teach a dog to beg at the table—the only way to teach a dog to beg at the table is to give him food from the table. In training, rewarding the dog with a food treat will help him associate praise and the treats with learning new behaviors that obviously please his owner.

TRAINING BEGINS: ASK THE DOG A QUESTION
In order to teach your dog anything, you must first get his attention. After all, he cannot learn anything if he is looking away from you with his mind on something else. To get his attention, ask him "School?" and immediately walk over to him and give him a treat as you tell him "Good dog." Wait a minute or two and repeat the routine, this time with a treat in your hand as you approach within a foot of the dog. Do not

go directly to him, but stop about a foot short of him and hold out the treat as you ask "School?" He will see you approaching with a treat in your hand and most likely begin walking toward you. As you meet, give him the treat and praise again.

The third time, ask the question, have a treat in your hand and walk only a short distance toward the dog so that he must walk almost all the way to you. As he reaches you, give him the treat and praise again. By this time, the dog will probably be getting the idea that if he pays attention to you, especially when you ask that question, it will pay off in treats and fun activities for him. In other words, he learns that "school" means doing fun things with you that result in treats and positive attention for him.

Remember that the dog does not understand your verbal language, he only recognizes sounds. Your question translates to a series of sounds for him, and those sounds become the

When initiating a training routine, use the leash to keep the puppy close and attentive, and a treat to keep him focused on you.

Food rewards make training much easier. Most dogs are motivated by the smell of a tasty treat, so owners can use this to their advantage. Fortunately, Shelties are eager to please and enjoy learning.

signal to go to you and pay attention; if he does, he will get to interact with you plus receive treats and praise.

THE BASIC COMMANDS

TEACHING SIT

Now that you have the dog's attention, attach his leash and hold it in your left hand and a food treat in your right. Place

Teaching your Sheltie to sit and stay is simple. Note that the trainer has her foot on the leash to keep control of the dog.

your food hand at the dog's nose and let him lick the treat but not take it from you. Say "Sit" and slowly raise your food hand from in front of the dog's nose up over his head so that he is looking at the ceiling. As he bends his head upward, he will have to bend his knees to maintain his balance. As he bends his knees, he will assume a sit position. At that point, release the food treat and praise lavishly with comments such as "Good dog! Good sit!" Remember to always praise enthusiastically, because dogs relish verbal praise from their owners and feel so proud of themselves whenever they accomplish a behavior.

You will not use food forever in getting the dog to obey your commands. Food is only used to teach new behaviors, and once the dog knows what you want when you give a specific command, you will wean him off the food treats but still maintain the verbal praise. After all, you will always have your voice with you, and there will be many times when you have no food rewards but expect the dog to obey.

TEACHING DOWN
Teaching the down exercise is easy when you understand how the dog perceives the down position, and it is very difficult when you do not. Dogs perceive the down position as a submissive one, therefore teaching the down exercise using a forceful method can sometimes make the dog develop such a fear of the down that he either runs away when you say "Down" or he attempts to snap at the person who tries to force him down.

Have the dog sit alongside your left leg, facing in the same direction as you are. Hold the leash in your left hand and a food treat in your right. Now place your left hand lightly on the top of the dog's shoulders where they meet above the spinal cord. Do not push down on the dog's shoulders; simply rest your left hand there so you can guide the dog to lie down close to your left leg rather than

DOUBLE JEOPARDY
A dog in jeopardy never lies down. He stays alert on his feet because instinct tells him that he may have to run away or fight for his survival. Therefore, If a dog feels threatened or anxious, he will not lie down. Consequently, it is important to keep the dog calm and relaxed as he learns the down exercise.

to swing away from your side when he drops.

Now place the food hand at the dog's nose, say "Down" very softly (almost a whisper) and slowly lower the food hand to the dog's front feet. When the food hand reaches the floor, begin moving it forward along the floor in front of the dog. Keep talking softly to the dog,

Begin teaching the stay command from a close distance. As you and your Sheltie progress, you can increase the distance between the two of you.

saying things like, "Do you want this treat? You can do this, good dog." Your reassuring tone of voice will help calm the dog as he tries to follow the food hand in order to get the treat.

When the dog's elbows touch the floor, release the food and praise softly. Try to get the dog to maintain that down position for several seconds before you let him sit up again. The goal here is to get the dog to settle down and not feel threatened in the down position.

TEACHING STAY

It is easy to teach the dog to stay in either a sit or a down position. Again, we use food and praise during the teaching process as we help the dog to understand exactly what it is that we are expecting him to do.

To teach the sit/stay, start with the dog sitting on your left

OBEDIENCE SCHOOL

A basic obedience beginner's class usually lasts for six to eight weeks. Dog and owner attend an hour-long lesson once a week and practice for a few minutes, several times a day, each day at home. If done properly, the whole procedure will result in a well-mannered dog and an owner who delights in living with a pet that is eager to please and enjoys doing things with his owner.

side as before and hold the leash in your left hand. Have a food treat in your right hand and place your food hand at the dog's nose. Say "Stay" and step out on your right foot to stand directly in front of the dog, toe to toe, as he licks and nibbles the treat. Be sure to keep his head facing upward to maintain the sit position. Count to five and then swing around to stand next to the dog again with him

When teaching the stay command, you can use a hand signal as well as your verbal command.

dog when you leave him. When you do, use your left hand open with the palm facing the dog as a stay signal, much the same as the hand signal a police officer uses to stop traffic at an intersection. Hold the food treat in your right hand as before, but this time the food is not touching the dog's nose. He will watch the food hand and quickly learn that he is going to get that treat as soon as you return to his side.

When you can stand 3 feet away from your dog for 30 seconds, you can then begin building time and distance in both stays. Eventually, the dog can be expected to remain in the stay position for prolonged periods of time until you return to him or call him to you. Always praise lavishly when he stays.

TEACHING COME

If you make teaching "come" a fun experience, you should

on your left. As soon as you get back to the original position, release the food and praise lavishly.

To teach the down/stay, do the down as previously described. As soon as the dog lies down, say "Stay" and step out on your right foot just as you did in the sit/stay. Count to five and then return to stand beside the dog with him on your left side. Release the treat and praise as always.

Within a week or ten days, you can begin to add a bit of distance between you and your

"COME" . . . BACK
Never call your dog to come to you for a correction or scold him when he reaches you. That is the quickest way to turn a come command into "Go away fast!" Dogs think only in the present tense, and your dog will connect the scolding with coming to you, not with the misbehavior of a few moments earlier.

REAP THE REWARDS

If you start with a normal, healthy dog and give him time, patience and some carefully executed lessons, you will reap the rewards of that training for the life of the dog. And what a life it will be! The two of you will find immeasurable pleasure in the companionship you have built together with love, respect and understanding.

never have a student that does not love the game or that fails to come when called. The secret, it seems, is never to teach the word "come."

At times when an owner most wants his dog to come when called, the owner is likely upset or anxious and he allows these feelings to come through in the tone of his voice when he calls his dog. Hearing that desperation in his owner's voice, the dog fears the results of going to him and therefore either disobeys outright or runs in the opposite direction. The secret, therefore, is to teach the dog a game and, when you want him to come to you, simply play the game. It is practically a no-fail solution!

To begin, have several members of your family take a few food treats and each go into a different room in the house. Take turns calling the dog, and each person should celebrate the dog's finding him with a treat and lots of happy praise. When a person calls the dog, he is actually inviting the dog to find him and get a treat as a reward for "winning."

A few turns of the "Where are you?" game and the dog will figure out that everyone is playing the game and that each person has a big celebration awaiting the dog's success at locating them. Once he learns to love the game, simply calling out "Where are you?" will bring him running from wherever he is when he hears that all-important question.

The come command is recognized as one of the most impor-

"WHERE ARE YOU?"

When calling the dog, do not say "Come." Say things like, "Rover, where are you? See if you can find me! I have a biscuit for you!" Keep up a constant line of chatter with coaxing sounds and frequent questions such as "Where are you?" The dog will learn to follow the sound of your voice to locate you and receive his reward.

tant things to teach a dog, but there are trainers who work with thousands of dogs and never teach the actual word "come." Yet these dogs will race to respond to a person who uses the dog's name followed by "Where are you?" For example, a woman has a 12-year-old companion dog who went blind, but who never fails to locate her owner when asked, "Where are you?"

Children particularly love to play this game with their dogs. Children can hide in smaller places like a shower or bathtub, behind a bed or under a table. The dog needs to work a little bit harder to find these hiding places but, when he does, he loves to celebrate with a treat and a tussle with a favorite youngster.

TEACHING HEEL

Heeling means that the dog walks beside the owner without

Herding dogs excel at learning to walk alongside their owners, although some dogs tend to lead the way. Your Sheltie must learn to walk by your side, regardless of your pace, without exerting any pressure on his leash.

A Sheltie, properly trained to heel, will stop when you stop walking, and then sit at your side until you resume walking again.

natural instincts and intelligence.

Begin with holding the leash in your left hand as the dog sits beside your left leg. Move the loop end of the leash to your right hand but keep your left hand short on the leash so it keeps the dog in close next to you.

Say "Heel" and step forward on your left foot. Keep the dog close to you and take three steps. Stop and have the dog sit next to you in what we now call the heel position. Praise verbally, but do not touch the dog. Hesitate a moment and begin again with "Heel," taking three steps and stopping, at which point the dog is told to sit again.

Your goal here is to have the dog walk those three steps without pulling on the leash. When he will walk calmly beside you for three steps without pulling, increase the number of steps you take to five. When he will walk politely beside you while you take five steps, you can increase the length of your walk to ten steps. Keep increasing the length of your stroll until the dog will walk quietly beside you without pulling as long as you want him to heel. When you stop heeling, indicate to the dog that the exercise is over by verbally praising as you pet him and say "OK, good dog." The "OK" is used as a release word, meaning that the exercise is finished and the dog is free to relax.

pulling. Most Shelties have no problem whatsoever in learning to walk on a leash precisely at the owner's side. This is true for a herding dog that learns that the owner is the master and that he belongs by his master's side. While many dog owners struggle with this exercise, Sheltie owners should revel in their dog's

If you are dealing with a dog who insists on pulling you around, simply "put on your brakes" and stand your ground until the dog realizes that the two of you are not going anywhere until he is beside you and moving at your pace, not his. It may take some time just standing there to convince the dog that you are the leader and you will be the one to decide on the direction and speed of your travel.

Each time the dog looks up at you or slows down to give a slack leash between the two of you, quietly praise him and say, "Good heel. Good dog." Eventually, the dog will begin to respond and within a few days he will be walking politely beside you without pulling on the leash. At first, the training sessions should be kept short and very positive; soon the dog will be able to walk nicely with you for increasingly longer distances. Remember also to give the dog free time and the opportunity to run and play when you are done with heel practice.

WEANING OFF FOOD IN TRAINING

Food is used in training new behaviors. Once the dog understands what behavior goes with a specific command, it is time to start weaning him off the food treats. At first, give a treat after

> **HEELING WELL**
> Teach your dog to heel in an enclosed area. Once you think the dog will obey reliably and you want to attempt advanced obedience exercises such as off-leash heeling, test him in a fenced-in area so he cannot run away.

each exercise. Then, start to give a treat only after every other exercise. Mix up the times when you offer a food reward and the times when you offer only praise so that the dog will never know when he is going to receive both food and praise and when he is going to receive only praise. This is called a variable-ratio reward system and it proves successful because there is always the chance that the owner will produce a treat, so the dog never stops trying for that reward. No matter what, *always* give verbal praise.

OBEDIENCE CLASSES

It is a good idea to enroll in an obedience class if one is available in your area. If yours is a show dog, handling classes would be more appropriate. Many areas have dog clubs that offer basic obedience training as well as preparatory classes for obedience competition. There are also local dog trainers who offer similar classes.

At obedience trials, dogs can earn titles at various levels of competition. The beginning levels of competition include basic behaviors such as sit, down, heel, etc. The more advanced levels of competition include jumping, retrieving, scent discrimination and signal work. The advanced levels require a dog and owner to put a lot of time and effort into their training, and the titles that can be earned at these levels of competition are very prestigious.

OTHER ACTIVITIES FOR LIFE
Whether a dog is trained in the structured environment of a class or alone with his owner at home, there are many activities that can bring fun and rewards to both owner and dog once they have mastered basic control.

Teaching the dog to help out around the home, in the yard or on the farm provides great satisfaction to both dog and owner. In addition, the dog's help makes life a little easier for his owner and raises his stature as a valued companion to his family. It helps give the dog a purpose by occupying his mind and providing an outlet for his energy.

Backpacking is an exciting and healthy activity that the dog can be taught without assistance from more than his owner. The exercise of walking and climbing is good for man and dog alike, and the bond that they develop together is priceless. The rule of thumb is to never allow the dog to carry more than one-sixth of his body weight.

If you are interested in participating in organized competition with your Shetland Sheepdog, there are activities other than obedience in which you and your dog can become involved. Shelties naturally excel in herding tests and trials that are sponsored by breed clubs around the country. Agility is a popular and fun sport where dogs run through an obstacle course that includes various jumps, tunnels and other exercises to test the dog's speed and coordination. The owners run through the course beside their dogs to give commands and to guide them through the course. Although competitive, the focus is on fun—it's fun to do, fun to watch and great exercise. Shelties are familiar sights in agility trials; they are frequent competitors and *winners!*

OBEDIENCE BENEFITS
Taking your dog to an obedience school may be the best investment in time and money you can ever make. You will enjoy the benefits for the lifetime of your dog and you will have the opportunity to meet people who have similar expectations for their companion dogs.

SHETLAND SHEEPDOG

Dogs suffer from many of the same physical illnesses as people. They might even share many of the same psychological problems. Since people usually know more about human diseases than canine maladies, many of the terms used in this chapter will be familiar but not necessarily those used by veterinarians. We will use the term *x-ray*, instead of the more acceptable term *radiograph*. We will also use the familiar term *symptoms* even though dogs don't have symptoms, which are verbal descriptions of the patient's feelings; dogs have *clinical signs*. Since dogs can't speak, we have to look for clinical signs...but we still use the term *symptoms* in this book.

As a general rule, medicine is *practiced*. That term is not arbitrary. Medicine is a constantly changing art as we learn more and more about genetics, electronic aids (like CAT scans and MRIs) and daily laboratory advances. There are many dog maladies, like canine hip dysplasia, which are not universally treated in the same manner. For example, some veterinarians opt for surgery more often than others do.

SELECTING A QUALIFIED VET
Your selection of a vet should be based not only upon his personality and ability with pure-bred dogs but also upon his convenience to your home. You want a vet who is close because you might have emergencies or need to make multiple visits for treatments. You want a vet who has services that you might require such as a boarding kennel and grooming facilities, and of course a good reputation for ability and responsiveness. There is nothing more frustrating than having to wait to get a response from your veterinarian.

All vets are licensed and their diplomas and/or certificates should be displayed in their waiting rooms. All vets should be

Before you buy your Shetland Sheepdog, meet and interview the vets in your area. Take everything into consideration—discuss his background, specialties, fees, emergency policy, etc.

First Aid at a Glance

Burns
Place the affected area under cool water; use ice if only a small area is burnt.

Car accident
Move dog from roadway with blanket; seek veterinary aid.

Bee stings/Insect bites
Apply ice to relieve swelling; antihistamine dosed properly.

Shock
Calm the dog; keep him warm; seek immediate veterinary help.

Animal bites
Clean any bleeding area; apply pressure until bleeding subsides; go to the vet.

Nosebleed
Apply cold compress to the nose; apply pressure to any visible abrasion.

Spider bites
Use cold compress and a pressurized pack to inhibit venom's spreading.

Bleeding
Apply pressure above the area; treat wound by applying a cotton pack.

Antifreeze poisoning
Immediately induce vomiting by using hydrogen peroxide.

Heat stroke
Submerge dog in cold bath; cool down with fresh air and water; go to the vet.

Fish hooks
Removal best handled by vet; hook must be cut in order to remove.

Frostbite/Hypothermia
Warm the dog with a warm bath, electric blankets or hot water bottles.

Snake bites
Pack ice around bite; contact vet quickly; identify snake for proper antivenin.

Abrasions
Clean the wound and wash out thoroughly with fresh water; apply antiseptic.

 Remember: an injured dog may attempt to bite a helping hand from fear and confusion. Always muzzle the dog before trying to offer assistance.

capable of dealing with routine health issues as well as routine surgery such as neutering, stitching up wounds and docking tails for those breeds in which such is required for show purposes. There are, however, many veterinary specialties that require further studies and internships. There are specialists in heart problems (veterinary cardiologists), skin problems (veterinary dermatologists), teeth and gum problems (veterinary dentists), eye problems (veterinary ophthalmologists) and x-rays (veterinary radiologists), and vets who have specialties in bones, muscles or certain organs. When the problem affecting your dog is serious, it is not unusual or impudent to get another medical opinion, although it is courteous to advise the vets concerned about this. You might also want to compare costs among several vets. Sophisticated health care and veterinary services can be very costly. Don't be bashful about discussing these costs with your vet or his staff. It is not infrequent that important decisions are based upon financial considerations.

PREVENTATIVE MEDICINE

It is much easier, less costly and more effective to practice preventative medicine than to fight bouts of illness and disease. Properly bred puppies come from parents that were selected based upon their genetic-disease profiles. Their

Breakdown of Veterinary Income by Category

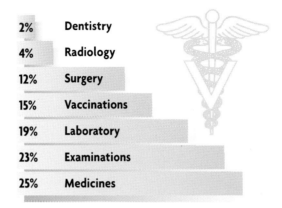

2%	Dentistry
4%	Radiology
12%	Surgery
15%	Vaccinations
19%	Laboratory
23%	Examinations
25%	Medicines

mother should have been vaccinated, free of all internal and external parasites and properly nourished. For these reasons, a visit to the veterinarian who cared for the dam is recommended. The dam can pass on disease resistance to her puppies, which can last for eight to ten weeks. She can also pass on parasites and many infections. That's why you should learn as much about the dam's health as possible.

A typical vet's income, categorized according to services performed. This survey dealt with small-animal (pets) practices.

WEANING TO FIVE MONTHS OLD

Puppies should be weaned by the time they are about two months old. A puppy that remains for at least eight weeks with his dam and littermates usually adapts better to other dogs and people later in his life.

Sometimes new owners have their puppy examined by a vet immediately, which is a good idea unless the pup is overtired by the journey home from the breeder. In that case, an appointment should be arranged for the next day.

The puppy will have his teeth examined and have his skeletal conformation and general health checked prior to certification by the vet. Puppies in certain breeds have problems with their kneecaps, cataracts and other eye problems, heart murmurs and undescended testicles. Your vet might have training in temperament evaluation. He will also set up a schedule for your pup's vaccinations.

VACCINATION SCHEDULING

Vaccination programs usually begin when the puppy is very young. Most vaccinations are given by injection and should only be done by a vet. Both he and you should keep a record of the date of the injection, the identification of

PUPPY VACCINATIONS

Your veterinarian will probably recommend that your puppy be fully vaccinated before you take him outside. There are airborne diseases, parasite eggs in the grass and unexpected visits from other dogs that might be dangerous to your puppy's health. Other dogs are the most harmful reservoir of pathogenic organisms, as everything they have can be transmitted to your puppy.

the vaccine and the amount given. Some vets give a first vaccination at six to eight weeks, but most dog breeders prefer the course not to commence until about ten weeks because of negating any antibodies passed on by the dam. The vaccination scheduling is usually based on a 15-day cycle. You must take your vet's advice as to when to vaccinate, as this may differ according to the vaccine used. Most vaccinations immunize your puppy against viruses.

The usual vaccines contain immunizing doses of several different viruses such as distemper, parvovirus, parainfluenza and hepatitis. There are other vaccines available when the puppy is at risk. You should rely upon professional advice. This is especially true for the booster-shot program. Most vaccination programs require a booster when the puppy is a year old and once a year thereafter. In some cases, circumstances may require more or less frequent immunizations. Canine cough, more formally known as tracheobronchitis, is treated with a vaccine that is sprayed into the dog's nostrils. Canine cough is usually included in routine vaccination, but this is often not so effective as for other major diseases.

FIVE MONTHS TO ONE YEAR OF AGE

Unless you intend to breed or show your dog, neutering the

Normal Shetland Sheepdog Skeleton

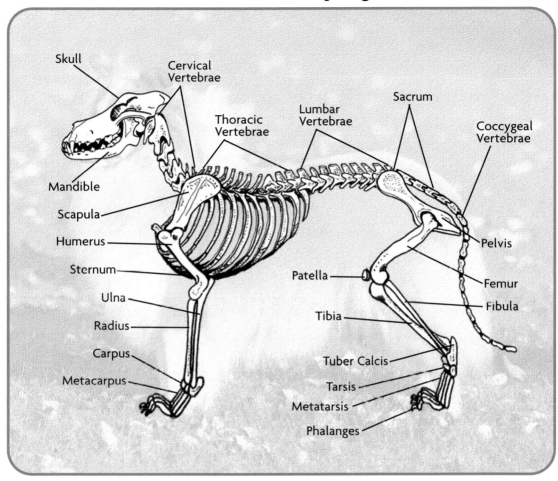

Skull

Cervical Vertebrae

Thoracic Vertebrae

Lumbar Vertebrae

Sacrum

Coccygeal Vertebrae

Mandible

Scapula

Humerus

Sternum

Ulna

Radius

Carpus

Metacarpus

Patella

Tibia

Tuber Calcis

Tarsis

Metatarsis

Phalanges

Pelvis

Femur

Fibula

puppy around six months of age is recommended. Discuss this with your vet. Most professionals advise neutering the puppy, but opinions can vary regarding the best age to have this done. Neutering (males) and spaying (females) have proven to be extremely beneficial. Besides eliminating the possibility of pregnancy, it inhibits (but does

MANY KINDS OF EARS
Not every dog's ears are the same. Ears that are open to the air are healthier than ears with poor air circulation. Sometimes a dog can have two differently shaped ears. You should not probe inside your dog's ears. Only clean that which is accessible with a cotton ball.

Age in Weeks:	6TH	8TH	10TH	12TH	14TH	16TH	20-24TH	52ND
Worm Control	✔	✔	✔	✔	✔	✔	✔	
Neutering							✔	
Heartworm		✔		✔		✔	✔	
Parvovirus	✔		✔		✔		✔	✔
Distemper		✔		✔		✔		✔
Hepatitis		✔		✔		✔		✔
Leptospirosis								✔
Parainfluenza	✔		✔		✔			✔
Dental Examination		✔					✔	✔
Complete Physical		✔					✔	✔
Coronavirus				✔			✔	✔
Canine Cough	✔							
Hip Dysplasia								✔
Rabies							✔	

Vaccinations are not instantly effective. It takes about two weeks for the dog's immune system to develop antibodies. Most vaccinations require annual booster shots. Your vet should guide you in this regard.

not prevent) breast cancer in bitches and prostate cancer in male dogs.

DOGS OLDER THAN ONE YEAR

Continue to visit the vet at least once a year. There is no such disease as old age, but bodily functions do change with age. The eyes and ears are no longer as efficient. Liver, kidney and intestinal functions often decline. Proper dietary changes, recommended by your vet, can make life more pleasant for the aging Shetland Sheepdog and you.

SKIN PROBLEMS IN SHETLAND SHEEPDOGS

Veterinarians are consulted by dog owners for skin problems more than for any other group of diseases or maladies. Dogs' skin is almost as sensitive as human skin and both can suffer from almost the same ailments (though the occurrence of acne in most dogs is rare). For this reason, veterinary dermatology has developed into a specialty practiced by many vets.

Since many skin problems have visual symptoms that are almost identical, it requires the skill of an experienced veterinary dermatologist to identify and cure many of the more severe skin disorders. Pet shops sell many treatments for skin problems, but most of the treatments are directed at symptoms and not the underlying problem(s). If your dog is suffering from a skin disorder, you should seek professional assistance as quickly as possible. As with all diseases, the earlier a problem is identified and treated, the more likely is the cure.

PARASITE BITES

Many of us are allergic to insect bites. The bites itch, erupt and may even become infected. Dogs have the same reaction to fleas, ticks and/or mites. When an insect lands on you, you have the chance to whisk it away with your hand. Unfortunately, when your dog is bitten by a flea, tick or mite, he can only scratch it away or bite it. By the time the dog has been bitten, the parasite has done some of its damage. It may also

DISEASE REFERENCE CHART

	What is it?	What causes it?	Symptoms
Leptospirosis	Severe disease that affects the internal organs; can be spread to people.	A bacterium, which is often carried by rodents, that enters through mucous membranes and spreads quickly throughout the body.	Range from fever, vomiting and loss of appetite in less severe cases to shock, irreversible kidney damage and possibly death in most severe cases.
Rabies	Potentially deadly virus that infects warm-blooded mammals.	Bite from a carrier of the virus, mainly wild animals.	1st stage: dog exhibits change in behavior, fear. 2nd stage: dog's behavior becomes more aggressive. 3rd stage: loss of coordination, trouble with bodily functions.
Parvovirus	Highly contagious virus, potentially deadly.	Ingestion of the virus, which is usually spread through the feces of infected dogs.	Most common: severe diarrhea. Also vomiting, fatigue, lack of appetite.
Canine cough	Contagious respiratory infection.	Combination of types of bacteria and virus. Most common: *Bordetella bronchiseptica* bacteria and parainfluenza virus.	Chronic cough.
Distemper	Disease primarily affecting respiratory and nervous system.	Virus that is related to the human measles virus.	Mild symptoms such as fever, lack of appetite and mucus secretion progress to evidence of brain damage, "hard pad."
Hepatitis	Virus primarily affecting the liver.	Canine adenovirus type I (CAV-1). Enters system when dog breathes in particles.	Lesser symptoms include listlessness, diarrhea, vomiting. More severe symptoms include "blue-eye" (clumps of virus in eye).
Coronavirus	Virus resulting in digestive problems.	Virus is spread through infected dog's feces.	Stomach upset evidenced by lack of appetite, vomiting, diarrhea.

have laid eggs to cause further problems in the near future. The itching from parasite bites is probably due to the saliva injected into the site when the parasite sucks the dog's blood.

Hereditary Skin Disorders

Veterinary dermatologists are currently researching a number of skin disorders that are believed to have a hereditary basis. These inherited diseases are transmitted by both parents, who appear (phenotypically) normal but have a recessive gene for the disease, meaning that they carry, but are not affected by, the disease. These diseases pose serious problems to breeders because in some instances there are no methods of identifying carriers. Often the secondary diseases associated with these skin conditions are even more debilitating than the skin disorders themselves, including cancers and respiratory problems.

Among the hereditary skin disorders, for which the mode of inheritance is known, are acrodermatitis, cutaneous asthenia (Ehlers-Danlos syndrome), sebaceous adenitis, cyclic hematopoiesis, dermatomyositis, IgA deficiency, color dilution alopecia and nodular dermatofibrosis. Some of these disorders are limited to one or two breeds, while others affect a large number of breeds. All inherited diseases must be diagnosed and treated by a veterinary specialist.

Auto-Immune Skin Conditions

Auto-immune skin conditions are commonly referred to as being allergic to yourself, while allergies are usually inflammatory reactions to an outside stimulus. Auto-immune diseases cause serious damage to the tissues that are involved.

The best known auto-immune disease is lupus, which affects people as well as dogs. The symptoms are variable and may affect the kidneys, bones, blood chemistry and skin. It can be fatal to both dogs and humans, though it is not thought to be transmissible. It is usually successfully treated with cortisone, prednisone or similar corticosteroid, but extensive use of these drugs can have harmful side effects.

HOT SPOTS/LICK GRANULOMA

Many dogs have a very poorly understood condition known as a lick granuloma or a hot spot. The manifestation of the problem is the dog's tireless attack at a specific area of the body, almost always the legs or paws. The dog licks so intensively that he removes the hair and skin, leaving an ugly, large wound. Owners who notice their dogs' biting and chewing at their extremities should have the vet determine the cause. If lick granuloma is the cause, although there is no absolute cure, corticosteroids are the most common treatment. Hot spots are common on coated breeds like the Shetland Sheepdog, especially during the summer months. Similar treatment is available through your vet.

AIRBORNE ALLERGIES

Just as humans have hay fever, rose fever and other fevers from which they suffer during the pollinating season, many dogs suffer the same allergies. When the pollen count is high, your dog might suffer, but don't expect him to sneeze and have a runny nose

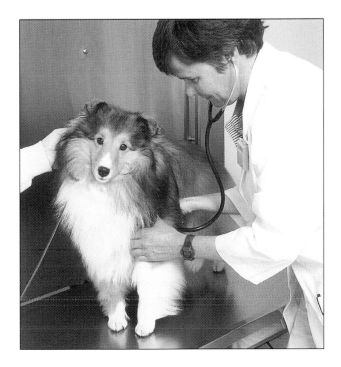

as a human would. Dogs react to pollen allergies the same way they react to fleas—they scratch and bite themselves. Dogs, like humans, can be tested for allergens. Discuss the testing with your veterinary dermatologist.

FOOD PROBLEMS

FOOD ALLERGIES

Dogs are allergic to many foods that are best-sellers and highly recommended by breeders and vets. Changing the brand of food that you buy may not eliminate the problem if the element to which the dog is allergic is contained in the new brand.

You should take your Sheltie to the veterinarian immediately if you detect something wrong with your dog.

Recognizing a food allergy is difficult. Humans vomit or have rashes when they eat a food to which they are allergic. Dogs neither vomit nor (usually) develop a rash. They react in the same manner as they do to an airborne or flea allergy: they itch, scratch and bite, thus making the diagnosis extremely difficult. While pollen allergies and parasite bites are usually seasonal, food allergies are year-round problems.

FOOD INTOLERANCE

Food intolerance is the inability of the dog to completely digest certain foods. For example, puppies that may have done very well on their mother's milk may not do well on cow's milk. The result of this food intolerance may be loose bowels, passing gas and stomach pains. These are the only obvious symptoms of food intolerance and that makes diagnosis difficult.

TREATING FOOD PROBLEMS

It is possible to handle food allergies and food intolerance yourself. Put your dog on a diet that he has never had. Obviously, if he has never eaten this new food, he can't yet have been allergic or intolerant

Especially in the warm months, coated breeds like Shelties can suffer from fleas, hot spots and other haircoat-related problems. Owners must check over their dogs carefully and be prepared to prevent and treat these problems.

of it. Start with a single ingredient that is not in the dog's diet at the present time. Ingredients like chopped beef or chicken are common in dog's diets, so try something else like fish, lamb, rabbit or some other source of animal protein. Keep the dog on this diet (with no additives) for a month. If the symptoms of food allergy or intolerance disappear, chances are your dog has a food allergy.

Don't think that the single ingredient cured the problem. You still must find a suitable diet and ascertain which ingredient in the old diet was objectionable. This is most easily done by adding ingredients to the new diet one at a time. Let the dog stay on the modified diet for a month before you add another ingredient. An alternative method is to carefully study the ingredients in the diet to which your dog is allergic or intolerant. Identify the main ingredient in this diet and eliminate the main ingredient by buying a different food that does not have that ingredient. Keep experimenting until the symptoms disappear after one month on the new diet.

BREED-SPECIFIC MEDICAL CONCERNS

Though Shetland Sheepdogs are hardy, long-lived dogs, the breed is subject to certain health conditions, some of which are hereditary. It behooves the potential puppy buyer to be aware of these problems and avoid them wherever possible. When you see a litter of Sheltie puppies, ask the breeder about these and any other health problems that occur in the breed.

Because of the Sheltie's heavy coat, skin problems can arise if coat care is neglected. Shelties need to be brushed daily to remove foreign matter and dead hair, which, if left in the coat, will cause matting. They don't need grooming by a professional groomer, but they must be brushed daily and bathed when necessary.

Eye problems such as PRA (progressive retinal atrophy), cataracts, ectasia syndrome and trichiasis are all seen in the breed. Have the puppy examined and tested by a veterinary ophthalmologist as early as eight to ten weeks of age to determine if the puppy is a candidate for these problems.

Hip dysplasia, epilepsy, thyroid deficiency, Collie nose (nasal dermatitis), deafness (particularly in blue merles) and von Willebrand's disease (blood-clotting disease) are well documented in the breed. Some of these problems are genetic and can be passed on to the puppy you buy. Today there are tests that can certify that the parents are free from the genes that cause these problems in the dogs and/or their offspring, and breeders do their best to eliminate any affected dogs and carriers from their breeding programs. Ask to see the parents' health clearances.

A male dog flea, *Ctenocephalides canis.*

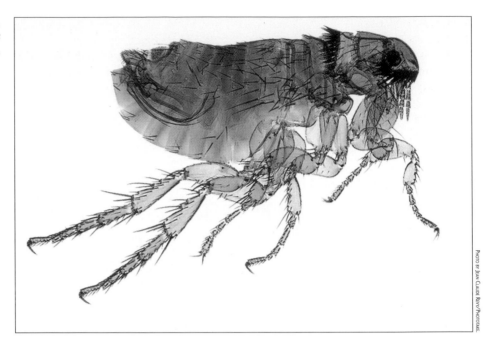

PHOTO BY JEAN CLAUDE REVY/PHOTOTAKE.

EXTERNAL PARASITES

FLEAS

Of all the problems to which dogs are prone, none is more well known and frustrating than fleas. Flea infestation is relatively simple to cure but difficult to prevent. Parasites that are harbored inside the body are a bit more difficult to eradicate but they are easier to control.

To control flea infestation, you have to understand the flea's life cycle. Fleas are often thought of as a summertime problem, but centrally heated homes have changed the patterns and fleas can be found at any time of the year. The most effective method of flea control is a two-stage approach: one stage to kill the adult fleas, and the other to control the development of pre-adult fleas. Unfortunately, no single active ingredient is effective against all stages of the life cycle.

FLEA KILLER CAUTION—"POISON"

Flea-killers are poisonous. You should not spray these toxic chemicals on areas of a dog's body that he licks, including his genitals and his face. Flea killers taken internally are a better answer, but check with your vet in case internal therapy is not advised for your dog.

LIFE CYCLE STAGES

During its life, a flea will pass through four life stages: egg, larva, pupa or nymph and adult. The adult stage is the most visible and irritating stage of the flea life cycle, and this is why the majority of flea-control products concentrate on this stage. The fact is that adult fleas account for only 1% of the total flea population, and the other 99% exist in pre-adult stages, i.e., eggs, larvae and nymphs. The pre-adult stages are barely visible to the naked eye.

THE LIFE CYCLE OF THE FLEA

Eggs are laid on the dog, usually in quantities of about 20 or 30, several times a day. The adult female flea must have a blood meal before each egg-laying session. When first laid, the eggs will cling to the dog's hair, as the eggs are still moist. However, they will quickly dry out and fall from the dog, especially if the dog moves around or scratches. Many eggs will fall off in the dog's favorite area or an area in which he spends a lot of time, such as his bed.

Once the eggs fall from the dog onto the carpet or furniture, they will hatch into larvae. This takes from one to ten days. Larvae are not particularly mobile and will usually travel only a few inches from where they hatch. However, they do have a tendency to move away from bright light and heavy

EN GARDE: CATCHING FLEAS OFF GUARD!
Consider the following ways to arm yourself against fleas:
- Add a small amount of pennyroyal or eucalyptus oil to your dog's bath. These natural remedies repel fleas.
- Supplement your dog's food with fresh garlic (minced or grated) and a hearty amount of brewer's yeast, both of which ward off fleas.
- Use a flea comb on your dog daily. Submerge fleas in a cup of bleach to kill them quickly.
- Confine the dog to only a few rooms to limit the spread of fleas in the home.
- Vacuum daily...and get all of the crevices! Dispose of the bag every few days until the problem is under control.
- Wash your dog's bedding daily. Cover cushions where your dog sleeps with towels, and wash the towels often.

traffic—under furniture and behind doors are common places to find high quantities of flea larvae.

The flea larvae feed on dead organic matter, including adult flea feces, until they are ready to change into adult fleas. Fleas will usually remain as larvae for around seven days. After this period, the larvae will pupate into protective pupae. While inside the pupae, the larvae will undergo

Photo by Dwight R. Kuhn

metamorphosis and change into adult fleas. This can take as little time as a few days, but the adult fleas can remain inside the pupae waiting to hatch for up to two years. The pupae are signaled to hatch by certain stimuli, such as physical pressure—the pupae's being stepped on, heat from an animal's lying on the pupae or increased carbon-dioxide levels and vibrations—indicating that a suitable host is available.

Once hatched, the adult flea must feed within a few days. Once the adult flea finds a host, it will not leave voluntarily. It only becomes dislodged by grooming or the host animal's scratching.

The adult flea will remain on the host for the duration of its life unless forcibly removed.

TREATING THE ENVIRONMENT AND THE DOG

Treating fleas should be a two-pronged attack. First, the environment needs to be treated; this includes carpets and furniture, especially the dog's bedding and areas underneath furniture. The environment should be treated with a household spray containing an Insect Growth Regulator (IGR) and an insecticide to kill the adult fleas. Most IGRs are effective against eggs and larvae; they actually mimic the fleas' own hormones and stop the eggs and larvae from developing into adult fleas. There are currently no treatments available to attack the pupa stage of the life cycle, so the adult insecticide is used to kill the newly hatched adult fleas before they find a host. Most IGRs are active for many months, while

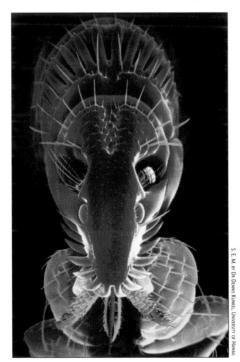

S. E. M. by Dr. Dennis Kunkel, University of Hawaii.

THE LIFE CYCLE OF THE FLEA

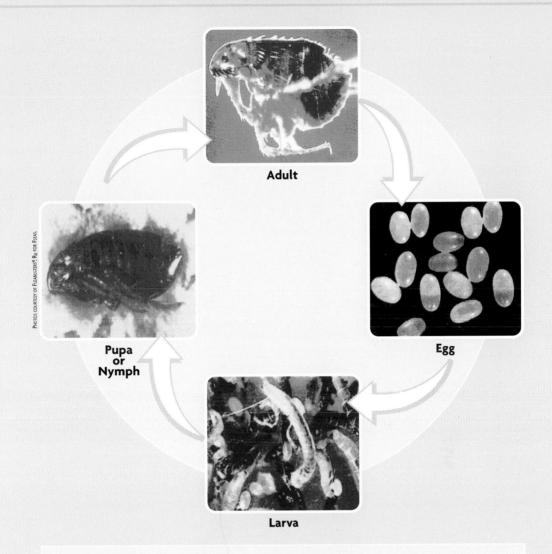

Adult

Egg

Larva

Pupa
or
Nymph

Fleas have been around for millions of years and have adapted to changing host animals. They are able to go through a complete life cycle in less than one month or they can extend their lives to almost two years by remaining as pupae or cocoons. They do not need blood or any other food for up to 20 months.

INSECT GROWTH REGULATOR (IGR)

Two types of products should be used when treating fleas—a product to treat the pet and a product to treat the home. Adult fleas represent less than 1% of the flea population. The pre-adult fleas (eggs, larvae and pupae) represent more than 99% of the flea population and are found in the environment; it is in the case of pre-adult fleas that products containing an Insect Growth Regulator (IGR) should be used in the home.

IGRs are a new class of compounds used to prevent the development of insects. They do not kill the insect outright, but instead use the insect's biology against it to stop it from completing its growth. Products that contain methoprene are the world's first and leading IGRs. Used to control fleas and other insects, this type of IGR will stop flea larvae from developing and protect the house for up to seven months.

The American dog tick, *Dermacentor variabilis*, is probably the most common tick found on dogs. Look at the strength in its eight legs! No wonder it's hard to detach them.

adult insecticides are only active for a few days.

When treating with a household spray, it is a good idea to vacuum before applying the product. This stimulates as many pupae as possible to hatch into adult fleas. The vacuum cleaner should also be treated with an insecticide to prevent the eggs and larvae that have been collected in the vacuum bag from hatching.

The second stage of treatment is to apply an adult insecticide to the dog. Traditionally, this would be in the form of a collar or a spray, but more recent innovations include digestible insecticides that poison the fleas when they ingest the dog's blood. Alternatively, there are drops that, when placed on the back of the dog's neck, spread throughout the hair and skin to kill adult fleas.

TICKS

Though not as common as fleas, ticks are found all over the tropical and temperate world. They don't bite, like fleas; they harpoon. They dig their sharp proboscis (nose) into the dog's skin and drink the blood. Their

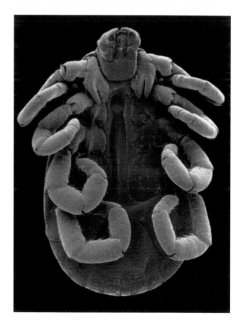

only food and drink is dog's blood. Dogs can get Lyme disease, Rocky Mountain spotted fever, tick bite paralysis and many other diseases from ticks. They may live where fleas are found and they like to hide in cracks or seams in walls. They are controlled the same way fleas are controlled.

The American dog tick, *Dermacentor variabilis*, may well be the most common dog tick in many geographical areas, especially those areas where the climate is hot and humid. Most dog ticks have life expectancies of a week to six months, depending upon climatic conditions. They can neither jump nor fly, but they can crawl slowly and can range up to 16 feet to reach a sleeping or unsuspecting dog.

MITES

Just as fleas and ticks can be problematic for your dog, mites can also lead to an itchy nuisance. Microscopic in size, mites are related to ticks and generally take up permanent residence on their host animal—in this case, your dog! The term *mange* refers to any infestation caused by one of the mighty mites, of which there are six varieties that concern dog owners.

Demodex mites cause a condition known as demodicosis

DEER-TICK CROSSING

The great outdoors may be fun for your dog, but it also is an home to dangerous ticks. Deer ticks carry a bacterium known as *Borrelia burgdorferi* and are most active in the autumn and spring. When infections are caught early, penicillin and tetracycline are effective antibiotics, but, if left untreated, the bacteria may cause neurological, kidney and cardiac problems as well as long-term trouble with walking and painful joints.

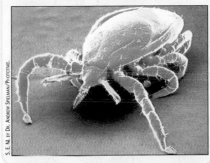

S. E. M. BY DR. ANDREW SPIELMAN/PHOTOTAKE.

PHOTO BY DR. DENNIS KUNKEL, UNIVERSITY OF HAWAII.

The head of an American dog tick, *Dermacentor variabilis*, enlarged and colorized for effect.

The mange mite, *Psoroptes bovis*, can infest cattle and other domestic animals.

PHOTO BY JAMES HAYDEN/YOAV/PHOTOTAKE

Human lice look like dog lice; the two are closely related.

PHOTO BY DWIGHT R. KUHN.

(sometimes called red mange or follicular mange), in which the mites live in the dog's hair follicles and sebaceous glands in larger-than-normal numbers. This type of mange is commonly passed from the dam to her puppies and usually shows up on the puppies' muzzles, though demodicosis is not transferable from one normal dog to another. Most dogs recover from this type of mange without any treatment, though topical therapies are commonly prescribed by the vet.

The *Cheyletiellosis* mite is the hook-mouthed culprit associated with "walking dandruff," a condition that affects dogs as well as cats and rabbits. This mite lives on the surface of the animal's skin and is readily transferable through direct or indirect contact with an affected animal. The dandruff is present in the form of scaly skin, which may or may not be itchy. If not treated, this mange can affect a whole kennel of dogs and can be spread to humans as well.

The *Sarcoptes* mite causes intense itching on the dog in the form of a condition known as scabies or sarcoptic mange. The cycle of the *Sarcoptes* mite lasts about three weeks, and the mites live in the top layer of the dog's skin (epidermis), preferably in areas with little hair. Scabies is highly contagious and can be passed to humans. Sometimes an allergic reaction to the mite worsens the severe itching associated with sarcoptic mange.

Ear mites, *Otodectes cynotis,* lead to otodectic mange, which most commonly affects the outer ear canal of the dog, though other areas can be affected as well. Dogs with ear-mite infestation commonly scratch at their ears, causing further irritation, and shake their heads. Dark brown droppings in the outer ear confirm the diagnosis. Your vet can prescribe a treatment to flush out the ears and kill any eggs in the ears. A complete month of treatment is necessary to cure the mange.

Two other mites, less common in dogs, include *Dermanyssus gallinae* (the poultry or red mite) and *Eutrombicula alfreddugesi* (the North American mite associated with trombiculidiasis or chigger infestation). The poultry mite frequently lives on chickens, but can transfer to dogs who spend time near farm animals. Chigger infestation affects dogs in the

NOT A DROP TO DRINK
Never allow your dog to swim in polluted water or public areas where water quality can be suspect. Even perfectly clear water can harbor parasites, many of which can cause serious to fatal illnesses in canines. Areas inhabited by water-fowl and other wildlife are especially dangerous.

Central US who have exposure to woodlands. The types of mange caused by both of these mites are treatable by vets.

INTERNAL PARASITES
Most animals—fishes, birds and mammals, including dogs and humans—have worms and other parasites that live inside their bodies. According to Dr. Herbert R. Axelrod, the fish pathologist, there are two kinds of parasites: dumb and smart. The smart parasites live in peaceful cooperation with their hosts (symbiosis), while the dumb parasites kill their hosts. Most worm infections are relatively easy to control. If they are not controlled, they weaken the host dog to the point that other medical problems occur, but they do not kill the host as dumb parasites would.

A brown dog tick, *Rhipicephalus sanguineus*, is an uncommon but annoying tick found on dogs.
PHOTO BY CAROLINA BIOLOGICAL SUPPLY/PHOTOTAKE.

DO NOT MIX
Never mix parasite-control products without first consulting your vet. Some products can become toxic when combined with others and can cause fatal consequences.

PHOTO BY CAROLINA BIOLOGICAL SUPPLY/PHOTOTAKE

The roundworm *Rhabditis* can infect both dogs and humans.

ROUNDWORMS

Average-size dogs can pass 1,360,000 roundworm eggs every day. For example, if there were only 1 million dogs in the world, the world would be saturated with thousands of tons of dog feces. These feces would contain around 15,000,000,000 roundworm eggs.

Up to 31% of home yards and children's sand boxes in the US contain roundworm eggs.

Flushing dog's feces down the toilet is not a safe practice because the usual sewage treatments do not destroy roundworm eggs.

Infected puppies start shedding roundworm eggs at three weeks of age. They can be infected by their mother's milk.

The roundworm, *Ascaris lumbricoides.*

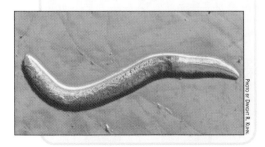

PHOTO BY DWIGHT R. KUHN.

ROUNDWORMS

The roundworms that infect dogs are known scientifically as *Toxocara canis*. They live in the dog's intestines and shed eggs continually. It has been estimated that a dog produces about 6 or more ounces of feces every day. Each ounce of feces averages hundreds of thousands of roundworm eggs. There are no known areas in which dogs roam that do not contain roundworm eggs. The greatest danger of roundworms is that they infect people, too! It is wise to have your dog tested regularly for roundworms.

In young puppies, roundworms cause bloated bellies, diarrhea, coughing and vomiting, and are transmitted from the dam (through blood or milk). Affected puppies will not appear as animated as normal puppies. The worms appear spaghetti-like, measuring as long as 6 inches. Adult dogs can acquire roundworms through coprophagia (eating contaminated feces) or by killing rodents that carry roundworms.

Roundworm infection can kill puppies and cause severe problems in adults, as the hatched larvae travel to the lungs and trachea through the bloodstream. Cleanliness is the best preventative for roundworms. Always pick up after your dog and dispose of feces in appropriate receptacles.

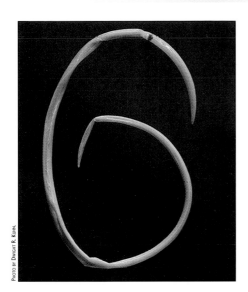

PHOTO BY DWIGHT R. KUHN.

HOOKWORMS

In the United States, dog owners have to be concerned about four different species of hookworm, the most common and most serious of which is *Ancylostoma caninum,* which prefers warm climates. The others are *Ancylostoma braziliense, Ancylostoma tubaeforme* and *Uncinaria stenocephala,* the latter of which is a concern to dogs living in the Northern US and Canada, as this species prefers cold climates. Hookworms are dangerous to humans as well as to dogs and cats, and can be the cause of severe anemia due to iron deficiency. The worm uses its teeth to attach itself to the dog's intestines and changes the site of its attachment about six times per day. Each time the worm repositions itself, the dog loses blood and can become anemic. *Ancylostoma caninum* is the most likely of the four species to cause anemia in the dog.

Symptoms of hookworm infection include dark stools, weight loss, general weakness, pale coloration and anemia, as well as possible skin problems. Fortunately, hookworms are easily purged from the affected dog with a number of medications that have proven effective. Discuss these with your vet. Most heartworm preventatives include a hookworm insecticide as well.

Owners also must be aware that hookworms can infect humans, who can acquire the larvae through exposure to contaminated feces. Since the worms cannot complete their life cycle on a human, the worms simply infest the skin and cause irritation. This condition is known as cutaneous larva migrans syndrome. As a preventative, use disposable gloves or a "poop-scoop" to pick up your dog's droppings and prevent your dog (or neighborhood cats) from defecating in children's play areas.

The hookworm, *Ancylostoma caninum.*

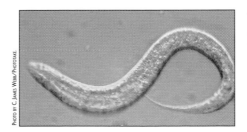

PHOTO BY C. JAMES WEBB/PHOTOTAKE.

The infective stage of the hookworm larva.

TAPEWORMS

Humans, rats, squirrels, foxes, coyotes, wolves and domestic dogs are all susceptible to tapeworm infection. Except in humans, tapeworms are usually not a fatal infection. Infected individuals can harbor 1000 parasitic worms.

Tapeworms, like some other types of worm, are hermaphroditic, meaning male and female in the same worm.

If dogs eat infected rats or mice, or anything else infected with tapeworm, they get the tapeworm disease. One month after attaching to a dog's intestine, the worm starts shedding eggs. These eggs are infective immediately. Infective eggs can live for a few months without a host animal.

The head and rostellum (the round prominence on the scolex) of a tapeworm, which infects dogs and humans.

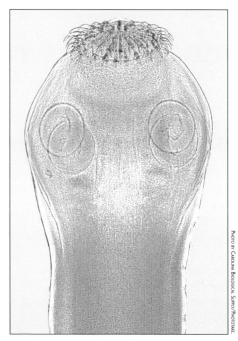

Photo by Carolina Biological Supply/Phototake

TAPEWORMS

There are many species of tapeworm, all of which are carried by fleas! The most common tapeworm affecting dogs is known as *Dipylidium caninum*. The dog eats the flea and starts the tapeworm cycle. Humans can also be infected with tapeworms—so don't eat fleas! Fleas are so small that your dog could pass them onto your hands, your plate or your food and thus make it possible for you to ingest a flea that is carrying tapeworm eggs.

While tapeworm infection is not life-threatening in dogs (smart parasite!), it can be the cause of a very serious liver disease for humans. About 50% of the humans infected with *Echinococcus multilocularis*, a type of tapeworm that causes alveolar hydatid, perish.

WHIPWORMS

In North America, whipworms are counted among the most common parasitic worms in dogs. The whipworm's scientific name is *Trichuris vulpis*. These worms attach themselves in the lower parts of the intestine, where they feed. Affected dogs may only experience upset tummies, colic and diarrhea. These worms, however, can live for months or years in the dog, beginning their larval stage in the small intestine, spending their adult stage in the large intestine and finally passing infective eggs through the dog's feces. The only way to detect whipworms is through a fecal examination, though this is not always foolproof. Treatment for whipworms is tricky, due to the worms' unusual life-cycle pattern, and very often dogs are reinfected due to exposure to infective eggs on the ground. The whipworm eggs can survive in the environment for as long as five years; thus, cleaning up droppings in your own backyard as well as in public places is absolutely essential for sanitation purposes and the health of your dog and others.

THREADWORMS

Though less common than round-worms, hookworms and those previously mentioned, thread-worms concern dog owners in the Southwestern US and Gulf Coast area where the climate is hot and humid. Living in the small intestine of the dog, this worm measures a mere 2 millimeters and is round in shape. Like that of the whipworm, the threadworm's life cycle is very complex and the eggs and larvae are passed through the feces. A deadly disease in humans, *Strongyloides* readily infects people, and the handling of feces is the most common means of transmission. Threadworms are most often seen in young puppies; bloody diarrhea and pneumonia are symptoms. Sick puppies must be isolated and treated immediately; vets recommend a follow-up treatment one month later.

HEARTWORM PREVENTATIVES

There are many heartworm preventatives on the market, many of which are sold at your veterinarian's office. These products can be given daily or monthly, depending on the manufacturer's instructions. All of these preventatives contain chemical insecticides directed at killing heartworms, which leads to some controversy among dog owners. In effect, heartworm preventatives are necessary evils, though you should determine how necessary based on your pet's lifestyle. There is no doubt that heartworm is a dreadful disease that threatens the lives of dogs. However, the likelihood of your dog's being bitten by an infected mosquito is slim in most places, and a mosquito-repellent (or an herbal remedy such as Wormwood or Black Walnut) is much safer for your dog and will not compromise his immune system (the way heartworm preventatives will). Should you decide to use the traditional preventative "medications," you can consider giving the pill every other or third month. Since the toxins in the pill will kill the heartworms at all stages of development, the pill would be effective in killing larvae, nymphs or adults, and it takes four months for the larvae to reach the adult stage. Thus, there is no rationale to poisoning the dog's system on a monthly basis. Lastly, do not give the pill during the winter months since there are no mosquitoes around to pass on their infection, unless you live in a tropical environment.

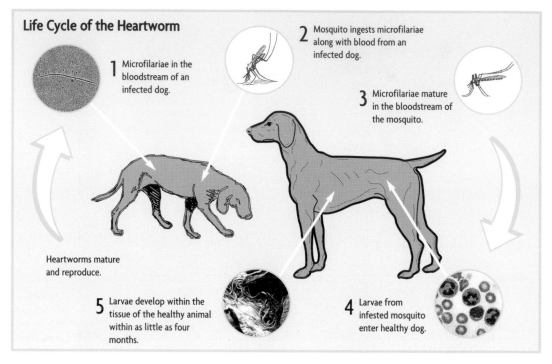

Life Cycle of the Heartworm

1 Microfilariae in the bloodstream of an infected dog.

2 Mosquito ingests microfilariae along with blood from an infected dog.

3 Microfilariae mature in the bloodstream of the mosquito.

Heartworms mature and reproduce.

5 Larvae develop within the tissue of the healthy animal within as little as four months.

4 Larvae from infested mosquito enter healthy dog.

HEARTWORMS

Heartworms are thin, extended worms up to 12 inches long, which live in a dog's heart and the major blood vessels surrounding it. Dogs may have up to 200 worms. Symptoms may be loss of energy, loss of appetite, coughing, the development of a pot belly and anemia.

Heartworms are transmitted by mosquitoes. The mosquito drinks the blood of an infected dog and takes in larvae with the blood. The larvae, called microfilariae, develop within the body of the mosquito and are passed on to the next dog bitten after the larvae mature. It takes two to three weeks for the larvae to develop to the infective stage within the body of the mosquito. Dogs are usually treated at about six weeks of age and maintained on a prophylactic dose given monthly.

Blood testing for heartworms is not necessarily indicative of how seriously your dog is infected. Although this is a dangerous disease, it is not easy for a dog to be infected. Discuss the various preventatives with your vet, as there are many different types now available. Together you can decide on a safe course of prevention for your dog.

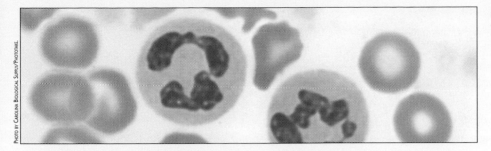

Magnified heartworm larvae, *Dirofilaria immitis.*

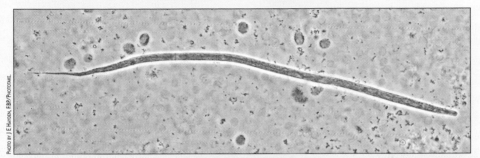

Heartworm, *Dirofilaria immitis.*

The heart of a dog infected with canine heartworm, *Dirofilaria immitis.*

Number-One Killer Disease in Dogs: CANCER

In every age, there is a word associated with a disease or plague that causes humans to shudder. In the 21st century, that word is "cancer." Just as cancer is the leading cause of death in humans, it claims nearly half the lives of dogs that die from a natural disease as well as half the dogs that die over the age of ten years.

Described as a genetic disease, cancer becomes a greater risk as the dog ages. Veterinarians and dog owners have become increasingly aware of the threat of cancer to dogs. Statistics reveal that one dog in every five will develop cancer, the most common of which is skin cancer. Many cancers, including prostate, ovarian and breast cancer, can be avoided by spaying and neutering our dogs by the age of six months.

Early detection of cancer can save or extend your dog's life, so it is absolutely vital for owners to have their dogs examined by a qualified vet or oncologist immediately upon detection of any abnormality. Certain dietary guidelines have also proven to reduce the onset and spread of cancer. Foods based on fish rather than beef, due to the presence of Omega-3 fatty acids, are recommended. Other amino acids such as glutamine have significant benefits for canines, particularly those breeds that show a greater susceptibility to cancer.

Cancer management and treatments promise hope for future generations of canines. Since the disease is genetic, breeders should never breed a dog whose parents, grandparents and any related siblings have developed cancer. It is difficult to know whether to exclude an otherwise healthy dog from a breeding program as the disease does not manifest itself until the dog's senior years.

RECOGNIZE CANCER WARNING SIGNS

Since early detection can possibly rescue your dog from becoming a cancer statistic, it is essential for owners to recognize the possible signs and seek the assistance of a qualified professional.

- Abnormal bumps or lumps that continue to grow
- Bleeding or discharge from any body cavity
- Persistent stiffness or lameness
- Recurrent sores or sores that do not heal
- Inappetence
- Breathing difficulties
- Weight loss
- Bad breath or odors
- General malaise and fatigue
- Eating and swallowing problems
- Difficulty urinating and defecating

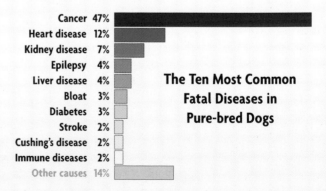

Cancer	47%
Heart disease	12%
Kidney disease	7%
Epilepsy	4%
Liver disease	4%
Bloat	3%
Diabetes	3%
Stroke	2%
Cushing's disease	2%
Immune diseases	2%
Other causes	14%

The Ten Most Common Fatal Diseases in Pure-bred Dogs

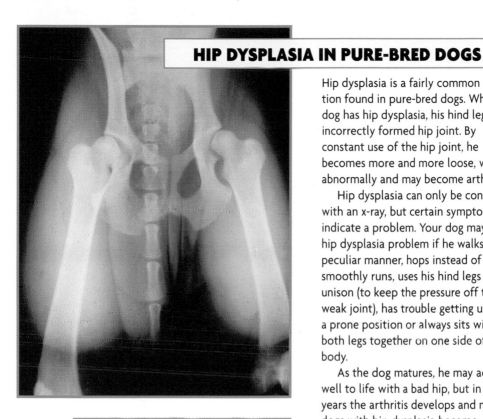

HIP DYSPLASIA IN PURE-BRED DOGS

Hip dysplasia is a fairly common condition found in pure-bred dogs. When a dog has hip dysplasia, his hind leg has an incorrectly formed hip joint. By constant use of the hip joint, he becomes more and more loose, wears abnormally and may become arthritic.

Hip dysplasia can only be confirmed with an x-ray, but certain symptoms may indicate a problem. Your dog may have a hip dysplasia problem if he walks in a peculiar manner, hops instead of smoothly runs, uses his hind legs in unison (to keep the pressure off the weak joint), has trouble getting up from a prone position or always sits with both legs together on one side of his body.

As the dog matures, he may adapt well to life with a bad hip, but in a few years the arthritis develops and many dogs with hip dysplasia become crippled.

Hip dysplasia is considered an inherited disease and can usually be diagnosed when the dog is three to nine months old, though two years of age is the benchmark for a dog to be definitely cleared as dysplasia-free. Some experts claim that a special diet might help your puppy outgrow the bad hip, but the usual treatments are surgical. The removal of the pectineus muscle, the removal of the round part of the femur, reconstructing the pelvis and replacing the hip with an artificial one are all surgical interventions that are expensive, but they are usually very successful. Follow the advice of your veterinarian.

Hip dysplasia is a badly worn hip joint caused by improper fit of the bone into the socket. It is easily the most common hip problem in larger dogs, but dogs of any breed can be affected by hip dysplasia. The illustration shows a healthy hip joint on the left and an unhealthy hip joint on the right.

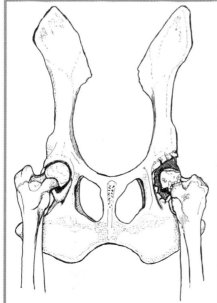

SHETLAND SHEEPDOG

The term *old* is a qualitative one. For dogs, as well as their masters, old is relative. Certainly we can all distinguish between a puppy Shetland Sheepdog and an adult Shetland Sheepdog—there are the obvious physical traits, such as size and coat, and personality traits. Puppies and young dogs like to play with children. Children's natural exuberance is a good match for the seemingly endless energy of young dogs. They like to run, jump, chase and retrieve. When dogs grow up and cease their interaction with children, they are often thought of as being too old to play with the kids.

On the other hand, if a Shetland Sheepdog is only exposed to people who lead more sedate lives, his life will normally be less active and the decrease in his activity level as he ages will not be as obvious.

Growing old happens to dogs just as it does to people. As with people, aging includes such manifestations as confusion, memory lapses, physical deterioration, pain, serious illnesses and even personality changes. The large breeds are usually considered seniors by 8 to 10 years of age. Smaller breeds often do not show signs of aging until they are 10 to 12 years old. Shelties follow this smaller-dog tendency by living into their mid-teens.

WHAT TO LOOK FOR IN SENIORS

Most veterinarians and behaviorists use around the eight-year mark as the time to consider a Sheltie a senior. The term *senior* does not imply that the dog is geriatric and has begun to fail in mind and body. Aging is essentially a slowing process. Humans

GETTING OLD

The bottom line is simply that your dog is getting old when *you* think he is getting old because he slows down in his level of general activity, including walking, running, eating, jumping and retrieving. On the other hand, the frequency of certain activities increases, such as more sleeping, more barking and more repetition of habits like going to the door without being called when you put your coat on to leave the house.

CDS: COGNITIVE DYSFUNCTION SYNDROME
"Old-Dog Syndrome"

There are many ways for you to evaluate old-dog syndrome. Veterinarians have defined CDS (cognitive dysfunction syndrome) as the gradual deterioration of cognitive abilities. These are indicated by changes in the dog's behavior. When a dog changes his routine response, and maladies have been eliminated as the cause of these behavioral changes, then CDS is the usual diagnosis.

More than half the dogs over eight years old suffer from some form of CDS. The older the dog, the more chance he has of suffering from CDS. In humans, doctors often dismiss the CDS behavioral changes as part of "winding down."

There are four major signs of CDS: has frequent housebreaking accidents inside the home, sleeping much more or much less than normal, acting confused and failing to respond to social stimuli.

SYMPTOMS OF CDS

FREQUENT POTTY ACCIDENTS
- *Urinates in the house.*
- *Defecates in the house.*
- *Doesn't signal that he wants to go out.*

SLEEP PATTERNS
- *Moves much more slowly.*
- *Sleeps more than normal during the day.*
- *Sleeps less during the night.*

CONFUSION
- *Goes outside and just stands there.*
- *Appears confused with a faraway look in his eyes.*
- *Hides more often.*
- *Doesn't recognize friends.*
- *Doesn't come when called.*
- *Walks around listlessly and without a destination.*

FAILURE TO RESPOND TO SOCIAL STIMULI
- *Comes to people less frequently, whether called or not.*
- *Doesn't tolerate petting for more than a short time.*
- *Doesn't come to the door when you return home.*

SENIOR SIGNS

An old dog starts to show one or more of the following symptoms:

- The hair on the face and paws starts to turn gray. The color breakdown usually starts around the eyes and mouth.
- Sleep patterns are deeper and longer, and the old dog is harder to awaken.
- Food intake diminishes.
- Responses to calls, whistles and other signals are ignored more and more.
- Eye contact does not evoke tail wagging (assuming it once did).

As your Sheltie enters his golden years, he deserves all the comforts of home. It may be time to surrender a cozy spot on the couch to your old friend.

readily admit that they feel a difference in their activity level from age 20 to 30, and then from 30 to 40, etc. By treating the eight-year-old and older dog as a senior, owners are able to implement certain therapeutic and preventative medical strategies with the help of their vets. A senior-care program should include at least two veterinary visits per year and screening sessions to determine the dog's health status, as well as nutritional counseling. Veterinarians determine the senior dog's health status through a blood smear for a complete blood count, serum chemistry profile with electrolytes, urinalysis, blood pressure check, electrocardiogram, ocular tonometry (pressure on the eyeball) and dental prophylaxis.

Such an extensive program for senior dogs is well advised before owners start to see the obvious physical signs of aging, such as slower and inhibited movement, graying, increased sleep/nap periods and disinterest in play and other activity. This preventative program promises a longer, healthier life for the aging dog. Among the physical problems common in aging dogs are the loss of sight and hearing, arthritis, kidney and liver failure, diabetes mellitus, heart disease and Cushing's disease (a hormonal disease).

In addition to the physical

WHEN YOUR DOG GETS OLD...
SIGNS THE OWNER CAN LOOK FOR

IF YOU NOTICE...	IT COULD INDICATE...
Discoloration of teeth and gums, foul breath, loss of appetite	Abcesses, gum disease, mouth lesions
Lumps, bumps, cysts, warts, fatty tumors	Cancers, benign or malignant
Cloudiness of eyes, apparent loss of sight	Cataracts, lenticular sclerosis, PRA, retinal dysplasia, blindness
Flaky coat, alopecia (hair loss)	Hormonal problems, hypothyroidism
Obesity, appetite loss, excessive weight gain	Various problems
Household accidents, Increased urination	Diabetes, kidney or bladder disease
Increased thirst	Kidney disease, diabetes mellitus
Change in sleeping habits, coughing	Heart disease
Difficulty moving	Arthritis, degenerative joint disease, spondylosis (degenerative spine disease)

IF YOU NOTICE ANY OF THESE SIGNS, AN APPOINTMENT SHOULD BE MADE IMMEDIATELY WITH A VETERINARIAN FOR A THOROUGH EVALUATION.

manifestations discussed, there are some behavioral changes and problems related to aging dogs. Dogs suffering from hearing or vision loss, dental discomfort or arthritis can become aggressive. Likewise, the near-deaf and/or blind dog may be startled more easily and react in an unexpectedly aggressive manner. Seniors suffering from senility can become more impatient and irritable. Housesoiling accidents are associated with loss of mobility,

kidney problems and loss of sphincter control as well as plaque accumulation, physiological brain changes and reactions to medications. Older dogs, just like young puppies, can suffer from separation anxiety, which can lead to excessive barking, whining, housesoiling and destructive behavior. Seniors may become fearful of everyday sounds, such as vacuum cleaners, heaters, thunder and passing traffic. Some dogs have difficulty sleeping, due to discomfort, the need for frequent potty visits and the like.

Owners should avoid spoiling the older dog with too many treats. Obesity is a common problem in older dogs and subtracts years from their lives. Keep the senior dog as trim as possible since excessive weight puts additional stress on the body's vital organs. Some breeders recommend supplementing the diet with foods high in fiber and lower in calories. Adding fresh vegetables and marrow broth to the senior's diet makes a tasty, low-calorie, low-fat supplement. Vets also offer specialty diets for senior dogs that are worth exploring.

Your dog, as he nears his twilight years, needs his owner's patience and good care more than ever. Never punish an older dog for an accident or abnormal behavior. For all the years of

NOTICING THE SYMPTOMS

The symptoms listed below are symptoms that gradually appear and become more noticeable. They are not life-threatening; however, the symptoms below are to be taken very seriously and warrant a discussion with your veterinarian:

• Your dog cries and whimpers when he moves, and he stops running completely.

• Convulsions start or become more serious and frequent. The usual convulsion (spasm) is when the dog stiffens and starts to tremble, being unable or unwilling to move. The seizure usually lasts for 5 to 30 minutes.

• Your dog drinks more water and urinates more frequently. Wetting and bowel accidents take place indoors without warning.

• Vomiting becomes more and more frequent.

EUTHANASIA

Euthanasia must be performed by a licensed veterinarian. There also may be societies for the prevention of cruelty to animals in your area. They often offer this service upon a vet's recommendation.

---

love, protection and companionship that your dog has provided, he deserves special attention and courtesies. The older dog may need to relieve himself at 3 a.m. because he can no longer hold it for eight hours. Older dogs may not be able to remain crated for more than two or three hours. It may be time to give up a sofa or chair to your old friend. Although he may not seem as enthusiastic about your attention and petting, he does appreciate the considerations you offer as he gets older.

Your Shetland Sheepdog does not understand why his world is slowing down. Owners must make the transition into the golden years as pleasant and rewarding as possible.

WHAT TO DO
WHEN THE TIME COMES

You are never fully prepared to make a rational decision about putting your dog to sleep. It is very obvious that you love your Shetland Sheepdog or you would not be reading this book. Putting a loved dog to sleep is extremely difficult. It is a decision that must be made with your vet. You are usually forced to make the decision when your dog experiences one or more life-threatening symptoms, making it necessary for you to seek veterinary help.

If the prognosis of the malady indicates the end is near and your beloved pet will only suffer more and experience no enjoyment for the balance of his life, then euthanasia is the right choice.

WHAT IS EUTHANASIA?

Euthanasia derives from the Greek, meaning *good death*. In other words, it means the planned, painless killing of a dog suffering from a painful, incurable condition, or who is so aged that he cannot walk, see, eat or control his excretory functions.

Euthanasia is usually accomplished by injection with an overdose of an anesthesia or barbiturate. Aside from the prick of the needle, the experience is usually painless.

MAKING THE DECISION

The decision to euthanize your dog is never easy. The days during which the dog becomes ill and the end occurs can be unusually stressful for you. If this is your first experience with the death of a loved one, you may need the comfort dictated by your religious beliefs. If you are the head of the family and have children, you should involve them in the decision of putting your Shetland Sheepdog to sleep. Usually your dog can be maintained on drugs for a few days at the vet's clinic in order to give you ample time to make a decision. During this time, talking with members of your family or even people who have lived through the same experience can ease the burden of your inevitable decision.

THE FINAL RESTING PLACE

Dogs can have some of the same privileges as humans. They can occasionally be buried in a pet cemetery, which is generally expensive, or, if they have died at home, can be buried in your yard in a place suitably marked with a stone or newly planted tree or bush. Alternatively, they can be cremated and the ashes returned to you, or some people prefer to leave their dogs at the vet's clinic.

All of these options should be discussed frankly and openly with your veterinarian. Do not be afraid

If you are interested in burying your dog, there are pet cemeteries catering to pet lovers.

to ask financial questions. Cremations can be individual, but a less expensive option is mass cremation, although of course the ashes cannot then be returned. Vets can usually arrange the cremation on your behalf and help you locate a pet cemetery.

GETTING ANOTHER DOG?

The grief of losing your beloved dog will be as lasting as the grief of losing a human friend or relative. In most cases, if your dog died of old age (if there is such a thing), he had slowed down considerably. Do you want a new Shetland Sheepdog puppy to replace him? Or are you better off finding a more mature Shetland Sheepdog, say two to three years of age, which will usually be house-trained and will have an already developed personality. In this case, you can find out if you like each other after a few hours of being together.

The decision is, of course, your own. Do you want another Shetland Sheepdog or perhaps a different breed so as to avoid comparison with your beloved friend? Most people usually stay with the same breed because they know and love the characteristics of that breed. Then, too, they often know people who have the same breed and perhaps they are lucky enough that a breeder they know expects a litter soon. What could be better?

Special gravestones and markers often indicate pets' graves; some graves may even be decorated with flowers or planted shrubs.

Cemeteries for pets usually have a place for funeral urns that contain the cremains of pets.

SHOWING YOUR
SHETLAND SHEEPDOG

When you purchase your Shetland Sheepdog, you will make it clear to the breeder whether you want one just as a lovable companion and pet, or if you hope to be buying a Shetland Sheepdog with show prospects. No reputable breeder will sell you a young puppy and tell you that it is *definitely* of show quality, for so much can go wrong during the

Like many other small-breed dogs, the Shetland Sheepdog is examined on the table by the show judge.

early months of a puppy's development. If you plan to show, what you will hopefully have acquired is a puppy with "show potential."

To the novice, exhibiting a Shetland Sheepdog in the show ring may look easy, but it takes a lot of hard work and devotion to do top winning at a show such as the prestigious Westminster Kennel Club dog show, not to mention a little luck too!

The first concept that the canine novice learns when watching a dog show is that each dog first competes against members of his own breed. Once the judge has selected the best member of each breed (Best of Breed), that chosen dog will compete with other dogs in his group. The Sheltie competes in the Herding Group. Finally, the dogs chosen first in each group will compete for Best in Show.

The second concept that you must understand is that the dogs are not actually compared against one another. The judge compares each dog against his breed standard, the written description of the ideal specimen that is approved by the American Kennel Club (AKC). While some early breed standards were indeed based on specific dogs that were famous or popular, many dedicated enthusiasts say that a perfect specimen, as described in the standard, has never walked into a show ring, has never been bred and, to the woe of dog breeders around the globe, does not exist. Breeders attempt to get as close to this ideal as possible with every litter, but theoretically the "perfect" dog is so elusive that it is impossible. (And if the "perfect" dog were born, breeders and judges would never agree that it was indeed "perfect.")

If you are interested in exploring the world of dog showing, your best bet is to join your local breed club or the national parent club, which is the American Shetland Sheepdog Association. These clubs often host both regional and national specialties, shows only for Shetland Sheepdogs, which can include conformation as well as obedience, agility and herding trials. Even if you have no intention of competing with your Sheltie, a specialty is like a festival for lovers of the breed who congregate to share their favorite topic: Shelties! Clubs also send out newsletters, and some organize training days and seminars in order that people may learn more about their chosen breed. To locate the breed club closest

The gait of the dog is evaluated by the judge as the handler moves the Sheltie around the ring.

to you, contact the AKC, which furnishes the rules and regulations for all of these events plus general dog registration and other basic requirements of dog ownership.

The American Kennel Club offers three kinds of conformation shows: an all-breed show (for all AKC-recognized breeds), a specialty show (for one breed only, usually sponsored by the parent club) and a Group show (for all breeds in the Group).

For a dog to become an AKC champion of record, the dog must accumulate 15 points at the shows from at least three different judges, including two "majors." A "major" is defined as a three-, four- or five-point win, and the number of points per win is determined by the number of dogs

If you are interested in dog shows, you can get valuable information and experience by visiting a local dog show or breed specialty. Breed clubs host shows especially for their breed.

entered in the show on that day. Depending on the breed, the number of points that are awarded varies. In a breed as popular as the Shetland Sheepdog, more dogs are needed to rack up the points. At any dog show, only one dog and one bitch of each breed can win points.

Dog showing does not offer "co-ed" classes. Dogs and bitches never compete against each other in the classes. Non-champion dogs are called "class dogs" because they compete in one of five classes. Dogs are entered in a particular class depending on age and previous show wins. To begin, there is the Puppy Class (for 6- to 9-month-olds and for 9- to 12-month-olds); this class is

followed by the Novice Class (for dogs that have not won any first prizes except in the Puppy Class or three first prizes in the Novice Class and have not accumulated any points toward their champion title); the Bred-by-Exhibitor Class (for dogs handled by their breeders or handled by one of the breeder's immediate family); the American-bred Class (for dogs bred in the US); and the Open Class (for any dog that is not a champion).

The judge at the show begins judging the Puppy Class, first dogs and then bitches, and proceeds through the classes. The judge places his winners first through fourth in each class. In the Winners Class, the first-place winners of each class compete with one another to determine Winners Dog and Winners Bitch. The judge also places a Reserve Winners Dog and Reserve Winners Bitch, which could be awarded the points in the case of a disqualification. The Winners Dog and Winners Bitch, the two that are awarded the points for the breed, then compete with any champions of record entered in the show. The judge reviews the Winners Dog, Winners Bitch and all of the champions to select his Best of Breed. The Best of Winners is selected between the Winners Dog and Winners Bitch. Were one of these two to be selected Best of

Breed, he or she would automatically be named Best of Winners as well. Finally the judge selects his Best of Opposite Sex to the Best of Breed winner.

At a Group show or all-breed show, the Best of Breed winners from each breed then compete against one another for Group One through Group Four. The judge compares each Best of Breed to his breed standard, and the dog that most closely lives up to the ideal for his breed is selected as Group One. Finally, all seven group winners (from the Herding Group, Toy Group, Hound Group, etc.) compete for Best in Show.

To find out about dog shows in your area, you can subscribe to the American Kennel Club's monthly magazine, the *American Kennel Gazette* and the accompanying *Events Calendar*. You can also look in your local newspaper for advertisements for dog shows in your area or go on the Internet to the AKC's website, www.akc.org.

If your Shetland Sheepdog is six months of age or older and registered with the AKC, you can enter him in a dog show where the breed is offered classes. Provided that your Shetland Sheepdog does not have a disqualifying fault, he can compete. Only unaltered dogs can be entered in a dog show, so if you have spayed or neutered your Shetland Sheepdog, your dog cannot compete in conformation

CLUB CONTACTS

You can get information about dog shows from the national kennel clubs:

American Kennel Club
5580 Centerview Dr., Raleigh, NC 27606-3390
www.akc.org

United Kennel Club
100 E. Kilgore Road, Kalamazoo, MI 49002
www.ukcdogs.com

Canadian Kennel Club
89 Skyway Ave., Suite 100, Etobicoke, Ontario
M9W 6R4, Canada
www.ckc.ca

The Kennel Club
1-5 Clarges St., Piccadilly, London
W1Y 8AB, UK
www.the-kennel-club.org.uk

If you have purchased a show-quality Sheltie and want to participate in a dog show, contact the American Kennel Club for information about future events. You will meet many wonderful folk who love the Sheltie as you do.

shows. The reason for this is simple. Dog shows are the main forum to prove which representatives of a breed are worthy of being bred. Only dogs that have achieved championships—the AKC "seal of approval" for quality in pure-bred dogs—should be bred. Altered dogs, however, can participate in other AKC events such as obedience trials and the Canine Good Citizen program.

Before you actually step into the ring, you would be well advised to sit back and observe the judge's ring procedure. The

MEET THE AKC

The American Kennel Club is the main governing body of the dog sport in the United States. Founded in 1884, the AKC consists of 500 or more independent dog clubs plus 4,500 affiliate clubs, all of which follow the AKC rules and regulations. Additionally, the AKC maintains a registry for pure-bred dogs in the US and works to preserve the integrity of the sport and its continuation in the country. Over 1,000,000 dogs are registered each year, representing about 150 recognized breeds. There are over 15,000 competitive events held annually for which over 2,000,000 dogs enter to participate. Dogs compete to earn over 40 different titles, from Champion to Companion Dog to Master Agility Champion.

judge asks each handler to "stack" the dog, hopefully showing the dog off to his best advantage. The judge will observe the dog from a distance and from different angles, and approach the dog to check his teeth, overall structure, alertness and muscle tone, as well as consider how well the dog "conforms" to the standard. Most importantly, the judge will have the exhibitor move the dog around the ring in some pattern that he should specify. Finally, the judge will give the dog one last look before moving on to the next exhibitor.

If you are not in the top four in your class at your first show, do not be discouraged. Be patient and consistent, and you may eventually find yourself in a winning line-up. Remember that

who designed a series of exercises after the Associated Sheep, Police Army Dog Society of Great Britain. Since the days of Mrs. Walker, obedience trials have grown by leaps and bounds, and today there are over 2,000 trials held in the US every year, with more than 100,000 dogs competing. Any AKC-registered dog can enter an obedience trial, regardless of conformational disqualifications or neutering.

Obedience trials are divided into three levels of progressive difficulty. At the first level, the Novice, dogs compete for the title

the winners were once in your shoes and have devoted many hours and much money to earn the placement. If you find that your dog is losing every time and never getting a nod, it may be time to consider a different dog sport or to just enjoy your Sheltie as a pet. Parent clubs offer other events, such as agility, obedience, herding and more, which may be of interest to the owner of a well-trained Shetland Sheepdog.

OBEDIENCE TRIALS
Obedience trials in the US trace back to the early 1930s when organized obedience training was developed to demonstrate how well dog and owner could work together. The pioneer of obedience trials is Mrs. Helen Whitehouse Walker, a Standard Poodle fancier,

FIVE CLASSES AT SHOWS
At most AKC all-breed shows, there are five regular classes offered: Puppy, Novice, Bred-by-Exhibitor, American-Bred and Open. The Puppy Class is usually divided as 6 to 9 months of age and 9 to 12 months of age. When deciding in which class to enter your dog, male or female, you must carefully check the show schedule to make sure that you have selected the right class. Depending on the age of the dog, previous first-place wins and the sex of the dog, you must make the best choice. It is possible to enter a one-year-old dog who has not won sufficient first places in any of the non-Puppy Classes, though the competition is more intense the further you progress from the Puppy Class.

Trainable, athletic and ever-ready for a challenge, Shelties regularly perform and excel in agility trials. They easily handle the collapsible tunnel.

PRACTICE AT HOME

If you have decided to show your dog, you must train him to gait around the ring by your side at the correct pace and pattern, and to tolerate being handled and examined by the judge. Most breeds require complete dentition, all breeds require a particular bite (scissors, level or undershot) and all males must have two apparently normal testicles fully descended into the scrotum. Enlist family and friends to hold mock trials in your yard to prepare your future champion!

Companion Dog (CD); at the intermediate level, the Open, dogs compete for the title Companion Dog Excellent (CDX); and at the advanced level, the Utility, dogs compete for the title Utility Dog (UD). Classes are sub-divided into "A" (for beginners) and "B" (for more experienced handlers). A perfect score at any level is 200, and a dog must score 170 or better to earn a "leg," of which three are needed to earn the title. To earn points, the dog must score more than 50% of the available points in each exercise; the possible points range from 20 to 40.

Each level consists of a different set of exercises. In the Novice level, the dog must heel on- and off-lead, come, long sit, long down and stand for examination. These skills are the basic ones required for a well-behaved "Companion Dog." The Open level requires that the dog perform the same exercises above but without a leash for extended lengths of time, as well as retrieve a dumbbell, broad jump and drop on recall. In the Utility level, dogs must perform ten difficult exercises, including scent discrimination, hand signals for basic commands, directed jump and directed retrieve.

Once a dog has earned the UD title, he can compete with other proven obedience dogs for the coveted title of Utility Dog Excellent (UDX), which requires that the dog win "legs" in ten shows. Utility Dogs who earn "legs" in Open B and Utility B earn points toward their Obedience Trial Champion title. In 1977 the title Obedience Trial Champion (OTCh.) was established by the AKC. To become an OTCh., a dog needs to earn 100 points, which requires three first places in Open B and Utility under three different judges.

The Grand Prix of obedience trials, the AKC National Obedience Invitational gives qualifying Utility Dogs the chance to win the newest and highest title: National Obedience Champion (NOC). Only the top 25 ranked obedience dogs, plus any dog ranked in the top 3 in his breed, are allowed to compete.

AGILITY TRIALS

Having had its origins in the UK back in 1977, AKC agility had its official beginning in the US in August 1994, when the first licensed agility trials were held. The AKC allows all registered breeds (including Miscellaneous Class breeds) to participate, providing the dog is 12 months of age or older. Agility is designed so that the handler demonstrates how well the dog can work at his side. The handler directs his dog over an obstacle course that includes jumps as well as tires, the dog walk, weave poles, pipe tunnels, collapsed tunnels, etc.

While working his way through the course, the dog must keep one eye and ear on the handler and the rest of his body on the course. The handler gives verbal and hand signals to guide the dog through the course.

The first organization to promote agility trials in the US was the United States Dog Agility Association, Inc. (USDAA), which was established in 1986 and spawned numerous member clubs around the country. Both the USDAA and the AKC offer titles to winning dogs. Three titles are available through the USDAA: Agility Dog (AD), Advanced Agility Dog (AAD) and Master Agility Dog (MAD). The AKC offers Novice Agility (NA), Open Agility (OA), Agility

This Sheltie demonstrates his skill as he navigates the weave poles.

Excellent (AX) and Master Agility Excellent (MX). Beyond these four AKC titles, dogs can win additional ones in "jumper" classes, Jumpers with Weave Novice (NAJ), Open (OAJ) and Excellent (MXJ), which lead to the ultimate title(s): MACH, Master Agility Champion. Dogs can continue to add number designations to the MACH titles, indicating how many times the dog has met the MACH requirements, such as MACH1, MACH2, etc.

Agility is great fun for dog and owner with many rewards for everyone involved. Interested owners should join a training club that has obstacles and experienced agility handlers who can introduce

Agility is a breeze for this nimble Sheltie who sails through the tire jump.

you and your dog to the "ropes" (and tires, tunnels, etc.).

HERDING TESTS AND TRIALS
Since the first sheepdog trials recorded in the late 19th century in Wales, the practice of herding trials has grown tremendously around the world. The first trial began as a friendly match to see which farmer's dog was the best at moving sheep. Today the sport is more organized than in those early days, and all herding breeds can earn titles at these fun and competitive events.

The AKC offers herding trials and tests to any herding dog that is nine months of age or older. The handler is expected to direct the Sheltie to herd various livestock, including sheep, ducks, goats and cattle. There are two titles for herding tests, Herding Tested (HT) and Pre-Trial Tested (PT). If the dog shows a basic innate ability, it is awarded the HT title; the PT title is awarded to a dog that can herd a small herd of livestock through a basic course.

In herding trials, there are four titles awarded: Herding Started (HS), Herding Intermediate (HI), Herding Excellent (HX) and Herding Champion (HCh.), the latter of which is awarded to a dog who has demonstrated mastery of herding in the most demanding of circumstances. Like shows, herding trials are judged against a set of standards as well as other dogs.

BEHAVIOR OF YOUR
SHETLAND SHEEPDOG

As a Shetland Sheepdog owner, you have selected your dog so that you and your loved ones can have a companion, a protector, a friend and a four-legged family member. You invest time, money and effort to care for and train the family's new charge. Of course, this chosen canine behaves perfectly! Well, perfectly like a *dog*.

THINK LIKE A DOG
Dogs do not think like humans, nor do humans think like dogs, though we try. Unfortunately, a dog is incapable of figuring out how humans think, so the responsibility falls on the owner to adopt a viable canine mindset. Dogs cannot rationalize, and they exist in the present moment. Many a dog owner makes the mistake in training of thinking that he can reprimand his dog for something the dog did a while ago. Basically, you cannot even reprimand a dog for something he did 20 seconds ago! Either catch him in the act or forget it! It is a waste of your and your dog's time—in his mind, you are reprimanding him for whatever he is doing at that moment.

The following behavioral problems represent some which owners most commonly encounter. Every dog is unique and every situation is unique. No author could purport for you to solve your Shetland Sheepdog's problem simply by reading a chapter. Here we outline some basic "dogspeak" so that owners' chances of solving behavioral problems are increased. Discuss bad habits with your veterinarian and he can recommend a behavioral specialist to consult in appropriate cases. Since behavioral abnormalities are the leading reason that owners abandon their pets, we hope that you will make a valiant effort to solve your Shetland Sheepdog's problem. Patience and understanding are virtues that must dwell in every pet-loving household.

DOGGIE DEMOCRACY
Your dog inherited the pack-leader mentality. He only knows about pecking order. He instinctively wants to be "top dog," but you have to convince him that you are boss. There is no such thing as living in a democracy with your dog. You are the one who makes the rules.

SEXUAL BEHAVIOR

Dogs exhibit certain sexual behaviors that may have influenced your choice of male or female when you first purchased your Shetland Sheepdog. To a certain extent, spaying/neutering will eliminate these behaviors, but if you are purchasing a dog that you wish to show or breed, you should be aware of what you will have to deal with throughout the dog's life.

Female dogs usually have two estruses per year with each season lasting about three weeks. These are the only times in which a female dog will mate, and she usually will not allow this until the second week of the cycle, but this does vary from bitch to bitch. If not bred during the heat cycle, it is not uncommon for a bitch to experience a false pregnancy, in which her mammary glands swell and she exhibits maternal tendencies toward toys or other objects.

Mounting, most often associated with males, is not merely a sexual expression but also one of dominance seen in males and females alike. Be consistent and persistent and you will find that you can "move mounters."

CHEWING

The national canine pastime is chewing! Every dog loves to sink his "canines" into a tasty bone, or whatever is available to chew, for that matter! Dogs need to chew, to massage their gums, to make their new teeth feel better and to exercise their jaws. This is a natural behavior deeply imbedded in all things canine. Your role as owner is not to stop the dog's chewing, but to redirect it to positive, chew-worthy objects. Be an informed owner and purchase safe chew toys like strong nylon bones that will not splinter. Be sure that the devices are safe and durable, since your dog's safety is at risk. Again, the owner is responsible for ensuring a dog-proof environment. The best answer is prevention: that is, put your shoes, handbags and other tasty objects in their proper

THE MIGHTY MALE

Males, whether castrated or not, will mount almost anything: a pillow, your leg or, much to your dismay, even your neighbor's leg. As with other types of inappropriate behavior, the dog must be corrected while in the act, which for once is not difficult. Often he will not let go! While a puppy is experimenting with his very first urges, his owners feel he needs to "sow his oats" and allow the pup to mount. As the pup grows into a full-size dog, with full-size urges, it becomes a nuisance and an embarrassment. Males always appear as if they are trying to "save the race," more determined and stronger than imaginable. While altering the dog at an appropriate age will limit the dog's desire, it usually does not remove it entirely.

It is vital to direct a Sheltie puppy's enthusiasm for play and merrymaking before he develops bad habits that are difficult to undo.

places (out of the reach of the growing canine mouth). Direct your puppy to his toys whenever you see him tasting the furniture legs or the leg of your pants. Make a loud noise to attract the pup's attention, and immediately escort him to his chew toy and engage him with the toy for at least four minutes, praising and encouraging him all the while.

Some trainers recommend deterrents, such as hot pepper or another bitter spice, or a product designed for this purpose, to discourage the dog from chewing unwanted objects. Test out these products with your own dog before investing in large quantities.

JUMPING UP

Jumping up is a dog's friendly way of saying hello! Some dog owners do not mind when their dog jumps up, which is fine for them. The problem arises when guests come to the house and the dog greets them in the same manner— whether they like it or not! However friendly the greeting may be, the chances are that your visitors will not appreciate your dog's enthusiasm. The dog will not be able to distinguish upon whom he can jump and whom he cannot. Therefore, it is probably best to discourage this behavior entirely.

Pick a command such as "Off" (avoid using "Down" since you will use that for the dog to lie down) and tell him "Off" when he jumps up. Place him on the ground on all fours and have him sit, praising him the whole time. Always lavish him with praise and petting when he is in the sit position. That way, you are still giving him a warm affectionate greeting, because you are as pleased to see him as he is to see you!

DIGGING

Digging, which is seen as a destructive behavior to humans, is actually quite a natural behavior in dogs. Although your Sheltie is not one of the "earth dogs" (also known as terriers), his desire to dig can be irrepressible and most frustrating. When digging occurs in your yard, it is actually a normal canine behavior redirected into something the dog can do in his everyday life. In the wild, a dog would be actively seeking food, making his own shelter, etc. He would be using his paws in a purposeful manner for his survival. Since you provide him with food and shelter, he has no need to use his paws for these purposes, and so the energy that he would be using may manifest itself in the form of little holes all over your yard and flower beds.

Perhaps your dog is digging as a reaction to boredom—it is somewhat similar to someone eating a whole bag of chips in front of the TV—because they are there and there is not anything better to do! Basically, the answer is to provide the dog with adequate play and exercise so that his mind and paws are occupied, and so that he feels as if he is doing something useful.

Of course, digging is easiest to control if it is stopped as soon as possible, but it is often hard to catch a dog in the act. If your dog is a compulsive digger and is not easily distracted by other activities, you can designate an area on your property where it is okay for him to dig. If you catch him digging in an off-limits area of the yard, immediately bring him to the approved area and praise him for digging there. Keep a close eye on him so that you can catch him in the act— that is the only way to make him understand what is permitted and what is not. If you take him to a hole he dug an hour ago and tell him "No," he will understand that you are not fond of holes, dirt or flowers. If you catch him while he

> ### DOWN, BOY!
> Stop a dog from jumping up before he jumps. If he is getting ready to jump onto you, simply walk away. If he jumps up on you before you can turn away, lift your knee so that it bumps him in the chest. Do not be forceful. Your dog soon will realize that jumping up is not a productive way of getting attention.

is stifle-deep in your tulips, that is when he will get your message.

BARKING

Dogs cannot talk—oh, what they would say if they could! Instead, barking is a dog's way of "talking." It can be somewhat frustrating because it is not always easy to tell what a dog means by his bark—is he excited, happy, frightened or angry? Whatever it is that the dog is trying to say, he should not be punished for barking. It is only when the barking becomes excessive, and when the excessive barking becomes a bad habit, that the behavior needs to be modified. Shetland Sheepdogs are rather vocal dogs, and they tend to use their barks to express many sentiments. This can be limited by discouraging excessive barking in a Sheltie pup through early training.

Keep in mind that some barking is desirable and purposeful, and some is not. If an intruder came into your home in the middle

Atop his perch, this well-trained Sheltie is surely "the king of the island."

of the night and your Shetland Sheepdog barked a warning, wouldn't you be pleased? You would probably deem your dog a hero, a wonderful guardian and protector of the home. However, if a friend drops by unexpectedly and rings the doorbell and is greeted with a sudden sharp bark, you would probably be annoyed at the dog. But in reality, isn't this just the same behavior? The dog does not know any better...unless he sees who is at the door and it is someone he knows, he will bark as a means of vocalizing that his (and your) territory is being threatened. While your friend is not posing a threat, it is all the same to the dog. Barking is his means of letting you know that there is an intrusion, whether friend or foe, on your property. This type of barking is instinctive and should not be discouraged.

Excessive habitual barking, however, is a problem that should be corrected early on. As your Shetland Sheepdog grows up, you will be able to tell when his barking is purposeful and when it is for no reason. You will become able to distinguish your dog's different barks and their meanings. For example, the bark when someone comes to the door will be different from the bark when he is excited

QUIET ON THE SET

To encourage proper barking, you can teach your dog the command "Quiet." When someone comes to the door and the dog barks a few times, praise him. Talk to him soothingly and, when he stops barking, tell him "Quiet" and continue to praise him. In this sense, you are letting him bark his warning, which is an instinctive behavior, and then rewarding him for being quiet after a few barks. You may initially reward him with a treat after he has been quiet for a few minutes.

to see you. It is similar to a person's tone of voice, except that the dog has to rely totally on tone of voice because he does not have the benefit of using words. An incessant barker will be evident at an early age.

There are some things that encourage a dog to bark. For example, if your dog barks non-stop for a few minutes and you give him a treat to quiet him, he believes that you are rewarding him for barking. He will associate barking with getting a treat, and will keep doing it until he is rewarded.

Begging is an easy behavior to avoid, but a difficult one to correct. Never give in to a dog that is begging at the table. Once you give in to a dog who begs, you will be living with a beggar for a lifetime.

FOOD STEALING

Is your dog devising ways of stealing food from your coffee table? If so, you must answer the following questions: Is your Shetland Sheepdog hungry or is he "constantly famished" like many dogs seem to be? Face it, some dogs are more food-motivated than others. Some dogs are totally obsessed by the smell of food and can only think of their next meal. Food stealing is terrific fun and always yields a great reward—*food*, glorious food.

Your goal, therefore, is to be sensible about where food is placed in the home, and to reprimand your dog whenever caught in the act of stealing. But remember, only reprimand the dog if you actually see him stealing, not later when the crime is discovered, for that will be of no use at all and will only serve to confuse.

BEGGING

Just like food stealing, begging is a favorite pastime of hungry puppies! It yields that same super reward—*food!* Dogs quickly learn that their owners keep the "good food" for themselves, and that we humans do not dine on dry food alone. Begging is a conditioned response related to a specific stimulus, time and place. The sounds of the kitchen, cans and bottles opening, crinkling bags, the smell of food in preparation, etc., will excite the dog and soon the paws are in the air!

Here is the solution to stopping this behavior: Never give in to a beggar! You are rewarding the dog for sitting pretty, jumping up, whining and rubbing his nose into you by giving him that glorious reward—food. By ignoring the dog, you will (eventually) force the behavior into extinction. Note that the behavior likely gets worse before it disappears, so be sure there are not any "softies" in the family who will give in to little "Oliver" every time he whimpers, "More, please."

SEPARATION ANXIETY

Your Shetland Sheepdog may howl, whine or otherwise vocalize his displeasure at your leaving the house and his being left alone. This is a normal reaction, no different from the child who cries as his mother leaves him on the first day at school. In fact, constant attention can lead to separation anxiety in the first place. If you are endlessly fussing over your dog, he will come to expect this from you all of the time and it will be more traumatic for him when you are not there. Obviously, you enjoy spending time with your dog, and he thrives on your love and attention. However, it should not become a dependent relationship where he is heartbroken without you.

One thing you can do to minimize separation anxiety is to make your entrances and exits as low-

"LONELY WOLF"
The number of dogs that suffer from separation anxiety is on the rise as more and more pet owners find themselves at work all day. New attention is being paid to this problem, which is especially hard to diagnose since it is only evident when the dog is alone. Research is currently being done to help educate dog owners about separation anxiety and how they can help minimize this problem in their dogs.

key as possible. Do not give your dog a long drawn-out goodbye, and do not lavish him with hugs and kisses when you return. This is giving in to the attention that he craves, and it will only make him miss it more when you are away. Another thing you can try is to give your dog a treat when you leave; this will not only keep him occupied and keep his mind off the fact that you have just left but it will also help him associate your leaving with a pleasant experience.

You may have to accustom your dog to being left alone in intervals. Of course, when your dog starts whimpering as you approach the door, your first instinct will be to run to him and comfort him, but do not do it! Eventually he will adjust and be just fine if you take it in small steps. His anxiety stems from being placed in an unfamiliar situation; by familiarizing him with being

PHARMACEUTICAL FIX

Veterinary scientists make daily advances toward the betterment and continued good health of our dogs. Discuss new drug therapies and treatment methods with your veterinarian and/or canine behaviorist.

There are two drugs specifically designed to treat mental problems in dogs. About seven million dogs each year are destroyed because owners can no longer tolerate their dogs' behavior, according to Nicholas Dodman, a specialist in animal behavior at Tufts University in Massachusetts.

The first drug, Clomicalm, is prescribed for dogs suffering from separation anxiety, which is said to cause them to react when left alone by barking, chewing their owners' belongings, drooling copiously or defecating or urinating inside the home.

The second drug, Anipryl, is recommended for cognitive dysfunction syndrome or "old dog syndrome," a mental deterioration that comes with age. Such dogs often seem to forget that they were housebroken and where their food bowls are, and they may even fail to recognize their owners.

A tremendous human-animal bonding relationship is established with all dogs, particularly senior dogs. This precious relationship deteriorates when the dog does not recognize his master. The drug can restore the bond and make senior dogs feel more like their "old selves."

alone he will learn that he is okay. That is not to say you should purposely leave your dog home alone but the dog needs to know that, while he can depend on you for his care, you do not have to be by his side 24 hours a day.

When the dog is alone in the house, he should be confined to his designated dog-proof area of the house. This should be the area in which he sleeps and already feels comfortable so he will feel more at ease when he is alone.

COPROPHAGIA

Feces eating is, to most humans, one of the most disgusting behaviors that their dog could engage in, yet to the dog it is perfectly normal. It is hard for us to understand why a dog would want to eat his own feces. He could be seeking certain nutrients that are missing from his diet, he could be just plain hungry or he could be attracted by the pleasing (to a dog) scent. While coprophagia most often refers to the dog eating his own feces, a dog may just as likely eat that of another animal as well if he comes across it. Dogs often find the stool of cats and horses more palatable than that of other dogs.

Vets have found that diets with a low digestibility, containing relatively low levels of fiber and high levels of starch, increase coprophagia. Therefore, high-fiber diets may decrease the likelihood of dogs' eating feces. Both the consistency of the stool (how firm it feels in the dog's mouth) and the presence of undigested nutrients increase the likelihood. Once the dog develops diarrhea from feces eating, it will likely quit this distasteful habit.

To discourage this behavior, first make sure that the food you are feeding your dog is nutritionally complete and that he is getting enough food. If changes in his diet do not seem to work, and no medical cause can be found, you will have to modify the behavior before it becomes a habit through environmental control. The best way to prevent your dog from eating his stool is to make it unavailable—clean up after he eliminates and remove any stool from the yard. If it is not there, he cannot eat it.

Your Sheltie relies on you for his care, continued safety and guidance. It is up to you to mold your Sheltie into a companion that behaves as beautifully as he looks.

SOUND BITES

When a dog bites, there is always a good reason for his doing so. Many dogs are trained to protect a person, an area or an object. When that person, area or object is violated, the dog will attack. A dog attacks with his mouth. He has no other means of attack.

Fighting dogs (the Sheltie is *not* one of these breeds) are taught to fight, but they also have a natural instinct to fight. This instinct is normally reserved for other dogs, though unfortunate accidents can occur; for example, when a baby crawls toward a fighting dog and the dog mistakes the crawling child as a potential attacker.

If a dog is a biter for seemingly no reason, if he bites the hand that feeds him or if he snaps at members of your family, see your veterinarian or behaviorist immediately to learn how to modify the dog's behavior.

INDEX

My Shetland Sheepdog

PUT YOUR PUPPY'S FIRST PICTURE HERE

Dog's Name _____

Date _____ Photographer _____